THE TERM STRUCTURE
OF INTEREST RATES

1961 Award Winners

THE FORD FOUNDATION DOCTORAL DISSERTATION SERIES

1960 Award Winners

Bernard H. Baum *Decentralization of Authority in a Bureaucracy*
Dissertation submitted to Department of Sociology, University of Chicago

Leon V. Hirsch *Marketing in an Underdeveloped Economy: The North Indian Sugar Industry*
Dissertation submitted to Graduate School of Business Administration, Harvard University

Bedros Peter Pashigian *The Distribution of Automobiles, An Economic Analysis of the Franchise System*
Dissertation submitted to Department of Economics, Massachusetts Institute of Technology

Martin Patchen *The Choice of Wage Comparison*
Dissertation submitted to Department of Social Psychology, University of Michigan

Fred M. Tonge *A Heuristic Program for Assembly Line Balancing*
Dissertation submitted to Graduate School of Industrial Administration, Carnegie Institute of Technology

1959 Award Winners

Kalman J. Cohen *Computer Models of the Shoe, Leather, Hide Sequence*
Dissertation submitted to Graduate School of Industrial Administration, Carnegie Institute of Technology

Bob R. Holdren *The Structure of a Retail Market and the Market Behavior of Retail Units*
Dissertation submitted to Department of Economics, Yale University

Frank Proschan *Polya Type Distributions in Renewal Theory, with an Application to an Inventory Problem*
Dissertation submitted to Department of Statistics, Stanford University

Andrew C. Stedry *Budget Control and Cost Behavior*
Dissertation submitted to Graduate School of Industrial Administration, Carnegie Institute of Technology

Victor H. Vroom *Some Personality Determinants of the Effects of Participation*
Dissertation submitted to Department of Psychology, University of Michigan

THE TERM STRUCTURE

OF INTEREST RATES

DAVID MEISELMAN

Assistant Professor,
Dept. of Economics,
The University of Chicago

PRENTICE-HALL, INC.

Englewood Cliffs, N. J.

To my parents

© — *1962 by* PRENTICE-HALL, INC.
Englewood Cliffs, N.J.

L. C. Catalog Card Number: 62:16454

Third printing .... *January, 1965*

• *Printed in the United States of America*
90678 — *C*

Foreword

This volume is one of five doctoral dissertations selected for publication in the third annual Doctoral Dissertation Competition sponsored by the Program in Economic Development and Administration of The Ford Foundation. The winning dissertations were completed during the academic year 1960–61 by doctoral candidates in business administration, the social sciences and other fields relevant to the study of problems of business.

The dissertation competition is intended to recognize and encourage excellence in research on business by graduate students. In specific pursuit of this aim, publication awards are made to persons recently granted doctorates in business whose dissertation research is especially distinguished by its analytical content and strong roots in underlying disciplines. To the same end, awards are made to a selected number of persons outside business schools who in their doctoral dissertations pursued with distinction interests relevant to the field of business.

The dissertations selected include, in addition to Dr. Meiselman's, the following:

Portfolio Selection: A Simulation of Trust Investment
> Geoffrey P. E. Clarkson
> Graduate School of Industrial Administration
> Carnegie Institute of Technology

The Investment Decision Under Uncertainty: Portfolio Selection
> Donald E. Farrar
> Faculty of Arts and Sciences
> Harvard University

An Evaluation of a Forced-Choice Differential Accuracy Approach to the Measurement of Supervisory Empathy
> Richard S. Hatch
> Department of Psychology
> University of Minnesota

Financing and Initial Operations of New Firms
George William Summers
Department of Management
Case Institute of Technology

On behalf of The Ford Foundation, I wish to express my gratitude to the members of the Editorial Committee for the care and thought they devoted to the selection process. The three members of this Committee, who made the final selection of winning dissertations, are: Professor Alex Bavelas of Stanford University, Professor Roy Blough of Columbia University, and Professor Robert Ferber of the University of Illinois.

The Editorial Committee's task was considerably lightened by the assistance of eleven readers, experts in the wide range of disciplines covered in the competition, who carefully screened the dissertations submitted. The Foundation joins the Committee in acknowledging their debt to Professors Paul Breer and Henry A. Landsberger of Cornell University, Richard M. Cyert of the Carnegie Institute of Technology, Robert B. Fetter of Yale University, Samuel Goldberg of Oberlin College, Albert H. Hastorf of Stanford University, Austin C. Hoggatt and Lyman W. Porter of the University of California (Berkeley), Daniel M. Holland of the Massachusetts Institute of Technology, John Neter of the University of Minnesota, and Harry V. Roberts of the University of Chicago.

Finally, my colleagues and I wish to acknowledge the important contribution of Prentice-Hall, Inc., to the publication of the selected dissertations.

Dyke Brown
Vice President
The Ford Foundation

New York, New York
January, 1962

Acknowledgments

This study was conducted while I was a member of the Money and Banking Workshop of the University of Chicago. It was supported by the Workshop under grants from The Ford Foundation and the Rockefeller Foundation. I benefitted greatly from participation in the Workshop and from the justifiably well-known zeal of its members for rigorous analysis and hypothesis testing. Their suggestions and criticisms were most helpful.

I am especially indebted to Milton Friedman, who first introduced me to the power of economic analysis. His encouragement and support made possible the completion of the study. I also received helpful comments from many who read drafts of the study, but notably from the other members of my dissertation committee, Martin Bailey and Lloyd Metzler, and from Lester Telser.

Muriel Porter cheerfully and accurately typed several drafts of the study. Lily Monheit assisted in the calculations.

The Oxford University Press kindly gave permission to quote liberally from *Value and Capital* by J. R. Hicks.

DAVID MEISELMAN

Contents

CHAPTER 3

RISK AVERSION
AND THE YIELD CURVE   *43*

APPENDIX A

MEASURING THE TERM STRUCTURE:
THE YIELD CURVE   *62*

APPENDIX B

PROBLEMS IN THE MEASUREMENT
OF AGGREGATE SHORT- AND LONG-TERM DEBT   *65*

APPENDIX C

SECULAR RELATIONSHIPS
BETWEEN U.S. SHORT- AND LONG-TERM RATES   *68*

BIBLIOGRAPHY   *72*

THE TERM STRUCTURE
OF INTEREST RATES

CHAPTER 1

The Term Structure:
A Futures Market in Loan Funds

1.1. The Term Structure Defined

The present market value of a default-free stream of payments, one that is expected to be received with certainty, is given by the familiar formula:

$$S = \frac{p_1}{(1 + R_1)} + \frac{p_2}{(1 + R_2)^2} + \cdots + \frac{p_n}{(1 + R_n)^n}$$

where $p_1, p_2, \ldots, p_n$ are payments in nominal dollars to be made at the ends of periods $1, 2, \ldots, n$, and where $R_1, R_2, \ldots, R_n$ are the rates of interest applicable to each payment expressed as a per cent per period. This is a study of the market determination of $R_1, R_2, \ldots, R_n$, the term-to-maturity structure of interest rates.

The present market value of a stream of future payments may also be affected by other variables if receipt of the payments stream $p_1, p_2, \ldots, p_n$ is uncertain. This study, however, is not concerned with that conceptually separate problem, that is, with the determination of the risk premium.[1] Uncertainty is not, however, entirely excluded because uncertainty about future interest rates may affect the value of $R_1, R_2, \ldots, R_n$. Many formulations of the present value formula assume that each element of the stream of default-free interest rates has the same value. This condition need not exist, and indeed, has typically not existed in the real world. When all interest rates are identical, that is, $R_1 = R_2 = \ldots$

---

[1] See Lawrence Fisher, "Determinants of the Risk Premiums on Corporate Bonds," *Journal of Political Economy*, 62 (June, 1959), 217–37 for an analysis of risk premiums.

$= R_n$, the rate of interest is invariant with respect to maturity. This "flat" yield curve characterizes only ten annual observations since 1900, the last of which was for 1930.[2]

The yields on bonds of different maturities are typically calculated with the aid of so-called bond tables.[3] The user of the bond tables knows the market price of the bond, S. He also knows the expected payments stream $p_1, p_2, \ldots, p_n$ from the coupon rate, the face amount of the bond, and the date of the terminal payment. The bond table, in effect, answers the question: "What is the one rate of interest which, when applied to the given payments stream, gives the existing market price of the security?" The rates, or yields, are then classified by maturity, that is, the length of time remaining before the terminal payment of the bond is to be made.

The single yield for the payments stream as a whole is then a weighted average of the individual R's. The weight of any one R, say, R_i, applicable to p_i, the payment to be made at the end of i periods in the future, depends on the relative contribution of p_i to the present value of the entire stream of payments. The relative contribution of any single payment can easily be seen from this present value formula; it varies directly with p_i and inversely with the ith root of unity plus R_i, where R is expressed as a per cent per period.

For example, consider two bonds maturing in ten years. Assume that one bond has a 3 per cent coupon, and will pay its holder $30 each year and a terminal payment at the end of ten years of $1,000. Assume that the other bond is a 10 per cent bond, and will pay its holder $100 each year in addition to the same final payment of $1,000. Both bonds are typically regarded as having ten years to maturity, yet the average term-to-maturity per dollar of the payments stream of the 10 per cent bond is shorter than it is for the 3 per cent bond. These considerations led Macaulay to suggest the substitution of a concept of "duration" for "maturity" to indicate the "longness" of the entire stream of payments of the bond taken as a whole.[4]

---

[2]See David Durand, *Basic Yields of Corporate Bonds, 1900–1942*, Technical Paper No. 3 (New York: National Bureau of Economic Research, 1942), Table 1, pp. 5–6.

[3]For example, see Charles E. Sprague, *Extended Bond Tables* (New York, 1909).

[4]See Frederick R. Macaulay, *The Movements of Interest Rates, Bond Yields, and Stock Prices in the United States Since 1856* (New York: National Bureau of Economic Research, 1938), Chap. 2, for an extensive discussion of the maturity duration problem.

These measurement problems, and several others discussed below,[5] introduce some lack of precision in the measurement and analysis of the term structure of interest rates. Fortunately, the lack of precision does not interfere with the main theoretical discussion or empirical findings of this study,[6] in part, because errors of measurement introduced by the maturity-duration problem tend to become smaller as the term of the bond becomes shorter. I shall return to this point when the principal model is introduced.[7]

1.2. The Yield Curve

Curves describing the structure of default-free interest rates as a function of term to maturity can have a wide variety of shapes. These curves are called yield curves. They are typically drawn with term to maturity along the horizontal axis and interest rates along the vertical axis. Two time series of yield curves have been estimated for the United States. One is based on market prices of corporate bonds; the other, on market prices of U.S. Treasury obligations. Though both attempt to measure essentially the same phenomenon, the two sets of yield curves tend to differ somewhat because they are derived from different data and by different methods.

This study uses mainly the yield curves derived from corporate bond data by David Durand.[8] (See Appendix A for a detailed discussion of methods and problems of estimating default-free interest rates classified by term to maturity.)

---

[5]See Appendix A.

[6]"The reader must not, from the above discussion, assume . . . 'yield' to be a useless concept . . . . The fact that a train makes a 100 mile run at an 'average' speed of 40 miles an hour is a piece of real information even if we know nothing about its speed at various times and places." Macaulay, *op. cit.*, p. 32.

[7]See Chap. 2.

[8]See David Durand, *op. cit.* Annual estimates for later years are found in David Durand and Willis J. Winn, *Basic Yields of Bonds, 1926–1947: Their Measurement and Pattern* Technical Paper No. 6 (New York: National Bureau of Economic Research, 1947), and *The Economic Almanac.* Durand has also attempted to estimate yield curves on a quarterly basis. See "A Quarterly Series of Corporate Basic Yields, 1952–1957, and Some Attendant Reservations," *The Journal of Finance,* **13**, 3, (September, 1958). Yield curves for U.S. Treasury securities are found in the *Treasury Bulletin.*

1.3. The Term Structure in a Futures Market in Loan Funds

The term structure of interest rates is determined in the market for loans of different maturities. It is useful to view this market as analogous to a commodity futures market, an analogy first used by Hicks in his discussion of interest rates in *Value and Capital*.[9]

The term structure of interest rates at any point in time contains an implicit set of forward or "futures" interest rates. The relationship between the term structure and the implicit forward rates is

$$1 + R_1 = 1 + r_1$$
$$(1 + R_2) = \sqrt[2]{(1 + r_1)(1 + r_2)}$$
$$(1 + R_3) = \sqrt[3]{(1 + r_1)(1 + r_2)(1 + r_3)}$$

$$\vdots \qquad \vdots$$

$$(1 + R_n) = \sqrt[n]{(1 + r_1)(1 + r_2) \ldots (1 + r_n)}$$

where $r_2, r_3, \ldots, r_n$ are the implicit forward rates at the beginning of period 1 for one period loans during periods 2, 3, ..., n respectively. These "short-term" forward rates, which can be calculated from the observed term structure, $R_1, R_2, \ldots, R_n$, represent the current market rates for one period loans in each of the future periods 2, 3, ..., n when all payments are made at the end of the loan.[10] Conversely, each observed "long-term" rate, $R_2, R_3, \ldots, R_n$, can be calculated from the current one period rate and the relevant number of successive forward one period rates. *This is not a statement of economic behavior.* It is a tautology.

The relationship between a given term structure of rates and the implied forward short-term rates is analogous to the well-known relationship between average and marginal quantities. Any long-term rate is an

---

[9]See J. R. Hicks, *Value and Capital,* 2nd ed. (London: Clarendon Press, 1946), Chaps. 11–13. For example, on p. 146 Hicks states, "These . . . are strictly analogous to the futures prices we discussed in the last chapter, and are determined in almost exactly the same way."

[10]Although the concepts remain the same, the arithmetic of these relationships becomes much more complicated when the assumption that all payments are made at the end of the loan is replaced by the assumption that each loan has a stream of coupon payments in addition to the terminal payment.

average of forward rates spanning the same period, and the forward rates are measures of the incremental costs or returns. For example, consider R_2 and R_3, the current rates on two-year and three-year single payment loans. A measure of the marginal cost of the three-year loan during year three alone is the forward rate, r_3. More generally, the current market rate for one period loans for any future period, say, period n, can be derived from

$$1 + r_n = \frac{(1 + R_n)^n}{(1 + R_{n-1})^{n-1}}$$

The implied forward short-term rate for any period is therefore higher than the corresponding market long-term rate when, in the neighborhood of this maturity, long-term rates are increasing with maturity. Also, implied forward short-term rates are lower than long-term rates when long-term rates are decreasing with maturity, and forward rates equal long-term rates when the yield curve is horizontal. Implied forward short-term rates can, of course, be higher than market long-term rates but be falling, and vice versa. Market interest rates that are a monotonic increasing function of maturity, a rising yield curve, imply that successive forward rates are higher than their corresponding long-term rates, but the forward rates need not also be monotonic increasing. They may, in fact, be irregularly rising and falling above the long rates.

The observed term structure implies not only these forward short-term rates, but also forward long-term rates. Each forward long-term rate is a function of the relevant number of successive short-term rates in the period spanned by the forward long-term rate, where unity plus the long-term rate is the geometric mean of the product of a set of terms each equal to one plus a one period forward rate, and it can be so calculated. For example, consider a 5 period loan running from period 7 through period 11. The present market rate for the loan is a function of $r_7, r_8, \ldots,$ r_{11}. The rate can be derived from

$$\sqrt[5]{\frac{(1 + R_{11})^{11}}{(1 + R_6)^6}}$$

where R_{11} is the yield to maturity of an 11 period loan and R_6 is the yield to maturity of a 6 period loan.

1.4. Speculation and Arbitrage

Although the futures market in loan funds does not have the same formal organization as the futures markets for commodities such as cotton or wheat, it is in essence similar. A market and a price exist today for wheat to be delivered next December; correspondingly, there is also, in principle, a present price for loan funds, or money, to be delivered for any length of time at any point in the future. For example, one can calculate the present returns from making a one-year loan three years in the future. These funds can now be loaned during the future one-year period at a currently known rate of interest by simultaneously buying a four-year bond and issuing a comparable three-year bond. The bond liability of the transactor will be repaid in three years, and at that time his portfolio will contain an asset of a bond with a current maturity of one year. In effect, the transactor is "short" on money to be delivered in three years, and "long" on four-year money.[11] Few, if any, such arrangements exist as a matter of descriptive reality. However, the identical result occurs when a transactor lengthens the maturity of his portfolio by selling a three-year bond and replacing it with a four-year bond. At the margin, the transactor is implicitly adding to his portfolio a one-year loan three years in the future. By the same token, when a transactor shortens the average maturity of his portfolio he is making a current marginal arrangement equivalent to borrowing in the future.

Forward rates net of transactions costs in a free market can have any values provided they are not negative. Were a forward rate to have a negative value, arbitrage would immediately drive up the rate to at least zero. Note that arbitrage is a combination of transactions yielding an assured return. Arbitrage does not consist of shifts among markets on the basis of current or expected yield differentials when complete certainty of profit is lacking. Such transactions are speculative.

Arbitrage between maturities can be illustrated by the following example. Assume simple interest and zero transaction costs. Also assume that the rate of interest on two-year loans, R_2, is 5 per cent per year, and that the rate of interest on a one-year loan for this year, R_1, is 12 per cent per year. This means that the forward rate on a one-year loan during year 2, r_2, is minus 2 per cent. Arbitrage profits can be realized by simul-

---

[11]This combination of transactions is analogous to a straddle in the commodity futures markets.

taneously borrowing at the two-year rate and lending at the one-year rate. An assured 2 per cent profit could still be obtained even if the one-year rate, one year hence, were to turn out to be zero per cent. Any positive interest rate on one-year loans, one year hence, would be added to the certain 2 per cent profit.

1.5. The Structure in a World of Certainty

Thus far I have developed the construct of the term structure as a set of prices in a futures market in loan funds. Let us now turn to an analysis of the operations of this futures market, first, in a world of certainty, and later, in greater detail in a world of uncertainty.

In a world of certainty, forward commodity prices and forward interest rates predict future prices and interest rates precisely. In fact, forward rates and future interest rates are identical. Thus, the equilibrium term structure under conditions of perfect certainty is solely a function of future interest rates because rates of return must be equal on all uses of wealth within any given period of time, although they need not be the same between periods. If, initially, any long-term rates were not the average of the relevant number of short-term rates described above, then assured profits could be realized by shifting among maturities up to the point where all long-term rates were the appropriate averages of the forward short-term rates they span. At this point no further profits can be made and there is no further incentive to shift. Conversely, a given structure in a world of perfect certainty accurately predicts all future and forward interest rates. A rising yield curve means that future interest rates will tend to be higher, and so forth.

1.6. The Structure in a World of Uncertainty: Speculation

Uncertainty, however, is the essence of the futures market in loan funds. In a world of uncertainty the transactor faces the futures market in loan funds with the same general alternatives he is confronted with in coping with uncertainty in commodity futures markets. The futures market in loan funds presents continuous opportunities for speculating in the term structure of interest rates. By speculation is meant the attempt to borrow at a low rate and lend at a high rate in the presence of uncertainty. For example, the professional speculator may buy bonds on margin, borrowing in the call money market to finance his acquisitions. Or, he may sell bonds short and use the proceeds of the sale to make very short-term loans. A bank or an insurance company may alter its portfolio by lengthening or shortening the maturities of its earning assets. A business may shift between the long-term market and the short-term market as a source of funds, and so forth.

1.7. The Structure in a World of Uncertainty: Hedging and Arbitrage

Transactors can also hedge against changes in interest rates. They can do so by employing the same general mechanism for hedging which is used in other markets. Hedging is achieved by having essentially the same item on both sides of one's balance sheet. The hedging mechanism operates through the identical response of an asset and an offsetting liability to the contingency hedged against so that net worth remains unchanged with respect to that contingency. To hedge against interest rate fluctuations, a transactor who acquires an asset must finance it with a liability that has a repayment stream matching the expected payments stream of the asset. Similarly, a transactor who incurs a liability can hedge against the consequences of a change in rates by acquiring an asset whose payments stream matches the liability's payment stream. In this way both sides of the balance sheet will respond alike to a given change in interest rates. To consider more specific examples, a person who buys a house and at the same time does not want to speculate on the future movement of interest rates can achieve this objective by financing the purchase with a long-term mortgage. A bank has very short-term liabilities in the form of deposits. It can avoid most speculation on interest rate changes by acquiring very short-term earning assets. A life insurance company has long-term liabilities in the form of commitments to deliver funds, on the average, in the distant future. The life insurance company can hedge against interest rate shifts by acquiring long-term assets, and so forth. Of course, none of these hedges is perfect. Few hedges and hedging mechanisms are perfect, which is to say that some "basis risk" typically exists.[12] In general, the hedging mechanisms avail-

---

[12]A basis risk occurs when a transactor wishing to hedge cannot arrange to have perfectly offsetting items on both sides of his balance sheet because potentially offsetting contracts or arrangements contain different specifications with respect to delivery date, quality, place of delivery, or the like.

able in the futures market for loan funds appear to be more imperfect than in many of the commodity markets because of the risk of default, the absence of the highly organized markets that characterize trading in many commodities, and the relatively longer periods of time spanned by loan hedges.[13]

In addition to speculating on interest changes, and trying to hedge against these changes, a transactor can also arbitrage loan funds between two points in time. The conditions under which arbitrage is possible have already been discussed, that is, when a forward interest rate is negative.

Alternative hypotheses of the determination of the term structure revolve about the central analytical and empirical problem of how the market copes with interest rate uncertainty. There are three major classes of hypotheses. Two depend crucially on expectations and flow from the empirical judgment that the market can best be analyzed as if it were dominated by transactors who speculate on future interest rates. The principal difference between the two is the treatment of risk aversion. One supposes indifference to uncertainty and behavior based on mathematical expectations alone. The other supposes risk aversion. The third class of hypotheses also depends on risk aversion, but these hypotheses presume that risk aversion leads to hedging against interest rate changes rather than speculating on them. The hedging behavior is the basis for market maturity preferences. All three classes of hypotheses will be discussed in more detail below.

1.8. Expectations Hypotheses: No Risk Aversion

Among hypotheses which assert that the term structure of interest rates depends on expectations of future interest rates, the hypothesis that has probably received the widest attention in recent years is that any long-term rate plus unity is a geometric mean of the product of a set of terms each equal to unity plus an expected short-term rate, the expected short-term rates covering the period spanned by the long-term rate in

---

[13]For another aspect of hedging which affects the financial markets see Reuben Kessel, "Inflation-Caused Wealth Redistribution: A Test of a Hypothesis," *American Economic Review*, **46** (March, 1956), for a discussion of the matching of real assets and real liabilities, and monetary assets and monetary liabilities to hedge against price level fluctuations.

question.[14] (For the sake of convenience, I shall call this *the* expectations hypothesis.) That a long-term rate is this average of the relevant number of forward short-term rates is a matter of arithmetic only. The expectations hypothesis adds economic content by asserting that forward rates, which are objective market phenomena, are unbiased estimates of expected future rates. If forward rates differ from anticipated rates, the hypothesis states that speculative shifts among maturities will drive the two sets of rates together. The analogous theory applied to the wheat market would assert that today's futures price for December wheat, for example, is equal to what the market today expects the price of comparable spot wheat to be in December and that the price of December wheat futures will change if and only if expectations regarding the price of spot wheat in December also change.

The expectations hypothesis follows from the assumptions that short- and long-term securities can be treated as if they were perfect substitutes and that transactors, indifferent to uncertainty and having similar expectations, equate the forward rates in the market to the expected rates. As a matter of descriptive reality, individual transactors may still speculate or hedge on the basis of risk aversion, but the speculators who are indifferent to uncertainty will bulk sufficiently large to determine market rates on the basis of their mathematical expectations alone.

Some implications of the expectations hypothesis follow from the equality of forward and expected rates. They have already been indicated in the preceding discussion of the certainty case. Because all forward rates are given by the term structure, at least in principle, all expected rates and yield curves can also be derived from the single term structure.

Although the expectations hypothesis has been widely accepted, it has been subject to increasing criticism in recent years.[15] The criticism clearly has some of its roots in the inability of economists to make the appealing theory operational. Many have felt that independent evidence

---

[14]For example, see Friedrich A. Lutz, "The Structure of Interest Rates," *Quarterly Journal of Economics*, **55** (1940–1941), pp. 36–63. Reprinted in American Economic Association, *Readings in the Theory of Income Distribution*, ed. by W. Fellner and Bernard Haley (Philadelphia: 1946).

[15]For example, J. M. Culbertson, "The Term Structure of Interest Rates, "*Quarterly Journal of Economics*, **71** (November, 1957), and D. G. Luckett, "Professor Lutz and the Structure of Interest Rates," *Quarterly Journal of Economics*, **73** (February, 1959).

of interest expectations was required to test the theory. With some exceptions, none exists.

The leading exception is an analysis of the response of call money rates and ninety-day loans to the well established seasonal variation of rates in the period before operations of the Federal Reserve System largely eliminated the seasonal variation in short-term rates. Both call loans and ninety-day loans were secured by the same New York Stock Exchange collateral. On the basis of the expectations hypothesis, the seasonal variation in call money rates should have been reflected in other interest rates, particularly rates on comparable paper of somewhat longer maturity. The ninety-day loans should have moved in anticipation of the known seasonal variation in call money. Macaulay compared the seasonal variation in the two series and found that the ninety-day seasonal did, in fact, move before the call money seasonal. However, it did not move enough. When seasonal influences were eliminated from the two series there was no evidence of successful forecasting.[16]

One survey of interest rate expectations has come to my attention. It was conducted early in 1943. The results of the one survey are not inconsistent with the expectations hypothesis, but the data leave much to be desired.[17]

---

[16]Frederick R. Macaulay, *The Movements of Interest Rates, Bond Yields, and Stock Prices in the United States Since 1856* (New York: National Bureau of Economic Research, 1938), pp. 33–36. He concludes that, ". . . an examination of the course of 'time' and 'call' money rates offers almost conclusive evidence that forecasting is really attempted and that at least one reason it is so badly done is that it is so difficult. . . . Bankers and brokers acted as if they knew virtually nothing about future cyclical or other non-seasonal movements of call money rates. They did know something about the seasonal fluctuations. What they knew about they were able to forecast, at least approximately; what they did not know about they were unable to forecast at all–except by accident."

[17]A survey conducted by Donald Woodward, then of the Mutual life Insurance Company of New York, is cited in an unpublished National Bureau study, W. Braddock Hickman, "The Interest Structure and War Financing" (National Bureau of Economic Research, 1943). Two hundred "experts" in various fields were polled and were asked to express their best judgments on the average rate of interest on Treasury obligations which might prudently be relied upon by a life insurance company for the next two decades. One hundred thirty-six replies were received, and 105 ventured forecasts. The modal forecast was that yields would not differ from the then current Treasury long-term yield of $2\frac{1}{2}$ per cent. There was substantial difference of opinion among the "experts" and the mean expected rate was 2.78 per cent. The yield curve in 1943 was a rising one as it had been before the Federal Reserve peg began in April, 1942. Thus, expectations of higher rates suggested by the survey are

Several investigators have attempted to assess the usefulness of applying the expectations hypothesis to the yield curve as a device to forecast interest rates. In an unpublished National Bureau study, Hickman compared forward rates and yield curves derived from the 1935–1942 yield curves with subsequent market interest rates during the 1935–1942 period and concluded that there was no correspondence between the actual rates and those forecast by the term structure.[18]

Culbertson, on the other hand, examined the alternative rates of return on holding long-term versus short-term Treasury securities to test the assertion of the expectations hypothesis that anticipated rates of return on all claims are equal for the same "holding period." He calculated the realized rates of return, including capital gains and losses, to investors who held either long-term Treasury bonds or Treasury bills for three-month holding periods and one-week holding periods during 1953. The realized rates of return were not equal. Culbertson interprets these results as contradicting the expectations hypothesis.[19]

Neither of these two exercises is a test of the expectations hypothesis. Anticipations may not be realized yet still determine the structure of rates in the manner asserted by the theory.

1.9. Expectations Hypotheses: Risk Aversion

The second class of expectations theories depends on risk aversion. These theories state that each forward rate is composed of two conceptually separate elements. These are (1) the expected rate, where "expected" is defined as the mathematical expectation, and (2) some positive risk or liquidity premium. Thus each forward rate is a biased estimate of the relevant expected future rate and is higher than the expected rate by the amount of the risk premium. The analogous theory applied to the wheat market would assert that today's future price for December wheat, for example, is equal to the sum of (1) what the market today expects the price of comparable spot wheat to be in December, plus (2) a risk premi-

---

consistent with the shape of the prevailing yield curve. The expectations hypothesis was not contradicted by the evidence cast up by the survey, but the single test is not a very powerful or conclusive one.

[18]W. Braddock Hickman, "The Term Structure of Interest Rates: An Exploratory Analysis" (New York: National Bureau of Economic Research, 1943), manuscript.

[19]Culbertson, *op. cit.*, p. 506.

um. In contrast with the expectations hypothesis, the theory implies that the price of December wheat futures will change if there is a change in either the mathematical expectation of the spot price or the risk premium and that the risk premium may change because of a change in either uncertainty or the disutility assumed to be associated with uncertainty. This is essentially the theory of "normal backwardation" developed by Keynes and Hicks which also has been applied to the market for loans.[20]

According to Hicks, short-term and long-term securities are not perfect substitutes. Risk aversion causes some borrowers to prefer to borrow for a long rather than a short period of time. In Hicks' words:

> Other things being equal, a person engaging in a long-term contract puts himself into a more risky position than he would be if he refrained from making it: but there are some persons (and concerns) for whom this will not be true, because they are already committed to needing loan capital over extensive future periods. They may be embarking on operations which take a considerable time to come to fruition; or they may merely be laying down plans for continuous production, in the form of long series of planned inputs and outputs, which it will not be easy to break off at any particular point. These persons will want to hedge their future supplies of raw materials. They will have a strong propensity to borrow long.[21]

Hicks then makes a casual but crucial empirical observation that, "On the other side of the market there does not seem to be any similar propensity . . . ," so that,

> the forward market for loans (like the forward market for commodities) may be expected to have a constitutional weakness on one side, a weakness which offers an opportunity for speculation. If no extra return is offered for long lending, most people (and institutions) would prefer to lend short, at least in the sense that they would prefer to hold their money on deposit in some way or other. But this situation would leave a large excess of demands to borrow long which would not be met. Borrowers would thus tend to offer better terms in order to persuade

---

[20]See J. M. Keynes, *A Treatise on Money*, Vol. II (London, 1930), pp. 353–73, and Hicks, *op. cit.*, pp. 135–140.

[21]Hicks, *op. cit.*, p. 146.

lenders to switch over into the long market (that is to say, enter the forward market). A lender who did this would be in a position exactly analogous to that of a speculator in a commodity market. He would only come into the long market because he expected to gain by so doing, and to gain sufficiently to offset the risk incurred.

The forward rate of interest for any particular future week . . . is thus determined . . . at that level which just tempts a sufficient number of 'speculators' to undertake the forward contract. It will have to be higher than the short rate expected by those speculators to rule in that week, since otherwise they would get no compensation for the risk they are incurring; it will, indeed, have to exceed it by a sufficient amount to induce the marginal speculator to undertake the risk. The forward rate will thus exceed the expected rate by a risk premium which corresponds exactly to 'normal backwardation' of the commodity markets. If short rates are not expected to change in the future, the forward rate will exceed the current short rate by the extent of the premium; if short rates are expected to rise, the excess will be greater than this normal level; it is only if short rates are expected to fall that the forward rates can lie below the current rate.

The same rules must apply to the long rates themselves, which . . . are effectively an average of the forward rates.[22]

Hicks thus holds that the futures market in loan funds can best be analyzed as if it were dominated by the lender's side of the market, where lenders are essentially speculators who have risk aversion, and who regard long loans as riskier than short loans. They therefore require compensation for providing borrowers with insurance, or hedges, against the consequences of interest rate changes. In effect, the lender's uncertainty equivalent is less than his mathematical expectation of future interest rates by the amount of the risk or illiquidity premium required to induce him to hold a longer-term security.

Hicks' analytical conclusions do not follow from his assumption of risk aversion. Lenders face the same uncertainty as borrowers and can, if they so prefer, also hedge against the consequences of interest rate fluctuations. The hedging mechanism for borrowers and lenders is identi-

---

[22]*Ibid.*, p. 147

cal and involves matching the expected payments streams of assets and liabilities. Contrary to Hicks' assertion, there are many institutions which appear to be hedgers in some degree and which have strong preferences for holding long-term assets. Among them are life insurance companies, and pension, endowment, and trust funds. Taken together they hold more financial assets than commercial banks and other institutions which appear to prefer holding short-term assets to hedge their short-term liabilities against some of the consequences of interest rate shifts.[23]

Institutions and individuals with long-term liabilities who seek to hedge must be induced to hold short-term claims by the payment of some premium. In the Hicksian model, the payment of such "insurance" premiums to long hedgers will make forward rates less rather than greater than expected market rates and "normal backwardation" will be negative. If a constitutional weakness does exist, it is not at all clear which side of the market is, or ought to be, the weak one. The *net* hedging position is the relevant variable, and net hedging can be either short or long. As is also the case in the commodity markets, the existence of risk aversion and hedging does not necessarily imply positive "normal backwardation" unless short-hedgers such as banks dominate. The relative importance of short and long hedging is an empirical matter that cannot be determined on any a priori basis.[24]

In addition, even if many individual borrowers are hedgers, it need not follow that the borrowing side of the market displays a preference for long-term funds. Some borrowers may speculate on future interest rates. For given expectations they will adjust their sources of funds sufficiently to offset some, or all, of any impact on the yield curve of the actions of the

---

[23]See Raymond Goldsmith, *Financial Intermediaries in the American Economy Since 1900* (Princeton, 1958). At the margin, however, many of these institutions may be acting on the basis of expectations so that cross-section or balance sheet data can be very misleading. A detailed analysis of institutional flows is required to determine the importance of hedging behavior *at the margin* by individual transactors.

[24]A long-hedger in the commodity markets is under contract to deliver commodities in the future and hedges his short position by going long, that is, purchasing a contract to have the identical commodity delivered to himself at the same time he is required to make delivery on his short commitment. In the loan market the transactor who is analogous to the commodity long-hedger is one who, like an insurance company, has a commitment to deliver funds in the far future. The life insurance company hedges by buying a long-term bond, which is essentially a contract to have funds delivered in the far future. A commercial bank is thus analogous to a short-hedger in the commodity markets.

hedging borrowers. The extent of their offsetting behavior will depend on their command over financial resources. If hedgers wish to borrow more long-term funds and by so doing initially drive up the long-term rate relative to the short, then the non-hedging borrowers, with given expectations, will shift out of long-term sources of funds to the shorter end of the market. The same analysis is relevant if preferences of transactors for short- or long-term borrowing or lending are based on considerations other than hedging. These may be legal restraints, fixed commitments, the Gurley-Shaw diversification demand, if one there is, and the like.

If, however, transactors with risk aversion dominate the market, it again is an empirical matter whether the short-hedgers or the long-hedgers will typically be the ones selling or buying the implied "insurance," and similarly it is also an empirical matter which class of hedgers typically sells "gambles" if transactors with risk preference dominate.

1.10. Risk Aversion and Hedging Only

Hedging behavior also depends on risk aversion. A transactor can either hedge or speculate. He will choose to hedge if (1) he is not specialized to bearing interest rate uncertainty, or (2) if the expected gains from speculation are not great enough to offset his distaste for uncertainty. Private borrowers and lenders will have schedules of preferences of demands or supplies of short-term and long-term funds as a function of the anticipated maturity composition of existing assets and liabilities and the opportunity costs of hedging, that is, alternative sources and uses of funds, which are claims or assets of other maturities. The spread between short- and long-term rates then depends on the excess demands or supplies of short- and long-term funds, or the net hedging pressure. The equilibrium structure of rates is determined at the combination of rates where all excess demands are zero.

Among the implications of this theory is that an increase in the demand for housing, a long-term asset, will lead to an increase in the demand for long-term mortgage funds, which in turn will drive up long-term relative to short-term rates. Similarly, a reduction in reserve requirements will tend to reduce short-term relative to long-term rates because banks are short-hedgers. Or, a change in the public debt policy to shorten maturities will drive up short-term relative to long-term rates, and so forth. There need be no "constitutional weakness" in this hedger dominated market. What is required for a pure hedging model is that where speculation does exist it be based on risk aversion and that the speculation not be important enough to affect rates.

CHAPTER 2

An Operational Test
of the Expectations Hypothesis

The first chapter was primarily devoted to a discussion of the term structure of interest rates as a futures market in loans and to the development of the principal hypotheses which seek to explain the term structure. This chapter is largely concerned with empirical tests of one of the hypotheses, the one I have called the expectations hypothesis.

Independent evidence of interest rate expectations is virtually unobtainable; and behavior based on these expectations is revealed only by the phenomena we seek to explain. How, then, can the theory be tested?

The expectations hypothesis need not be tested by relating yield curves to contemporaneous expectations. Instead, *changes* in, rather than *levels* of interest rates can be related to factors which systematically cause *revisions of expectations*. Other research has established some of the factors affecting expectations, and these can be applied to expectations of interest rates.

Recent research in a wide variety of behavioral contexts has indicated that hypotheses which assert that expectations tend to be related to past experience, often a weighted average of past experience, are consistent with the data.[1] Further, these hypotheses state that expectations tend

---

[1] For example, see Phillip Cagan, "The Monetary Dynamics of Hyperinflation," in Milton Friedman (ed.), *Studies in the Quantity Theory* (Chicago, 1956); Milton Friedman, *A Theory of the Consumption Function* (Princeton, 1957); Zvi Griliches, "The Demand for Fertilizer: An Economic Interpretation of a Technical Change," *Journal of Farm Economics*, **40** (August, 1958); L. M. Koyck, *Distributed Lags and Investment Analysis* (Amsterdam, 1954); Marc Nerlove, *Distributed Lags and Demand Analysis for Agricultural and Other Commodities* (U.S. Department of Agriculture, Agriculture Handbook No. 141: June, 1958).

to be systematically altered on the basis of new experience whenever unfolding events differ from what had been anticipated.

The same view of expectations can be applied to expectations of interest rates. In some respects the task of estimating expectations for purposes of testing the expectations hypothesis is made easier because, according to the theory we seek to test, expectations are already impounded and discounted in the term structure. Therefore, it is not necessary to examine a long chain of previous events in order to derive the state of expectations. Rather, we can observe the response of expectations to errors which have been made in forecasting actual market rates, again within the context of the theory being tested.

2.1. The Model

Consider the term structure at time t, where $_tR_{1t}, _tR_{2t}, \ldots, _tR_{nt}$ are the rates of interest on payments to be made at the ends of years $t, t + 1, \ldots, t + (n - 1)$. The forward rate on a one-year loan during the period $t + 1$ can easily be derived from the term structure by the method discussed above in Sec. 1.3.[2] This will be:

$$_{t+1}r_{1t} = \frac{(1 + {}_tR_{2t})^2}{(1 + {}_tR_{1t})} - 1$$

where $_{t+1}r_{1t}$ is the forward rate on a one-year loan during $t + 1$ derived from the structure existing at the beginning of period t. According to the expectations hypothesis, expected rates are equal to the forward rates given by the market. Thus, for purposes of testing the expectations hypothesis, $_{t+1}r_{1t}$ becomes the rate on the delivery of one-year loan funds expected at the beginning of period t to prevail at the beginning of the period $t + 1$.

---

[2]This study uses the following notation: capital letters represent actual market rates; lower case letters represent forward, implied, or expected rates; the duration of the loan is given by the first subscript; the prescript is the period in the beginning of which the rate in question becomes applicable; the second subscript gives the period at the beginning of which the rate is recorded in the market. Thus, $_{t+1}R_{30t+1}$ refers to the actual market rate of interest at the beginning of period $t + 1$ on a thirty-year loan commencing at the beginning of period $t + 1$. Also, $_{t+3}r_{2t}$ refers to the forward rate on a two-year loan starting at the beginning of period $t + 3$ which is implied by the market rates existing at the beginning of period t. Or, $_{1923}r_{61910}$ is the forward rate on a six-year loan to commence in 1923 implied by market rates at the beginning of 1910.

Similarly, at the beginning of the year t one can look back at the market rates prevailing one year earlier. From these rates one can derive the one-year rate that had been expected to prevail at the beginning of year t. The expected rate can then be compared with the actual market rate on one-year loans at the beginning of year t. If actual rates are higher than had been anticipated, then the market may systematically revise upward expectations of what short-term rates in the future are likely to be. Similarly, if actual rates are lower than had been anticipated, then the market may also systematically revise downward expectations of future short-term rates.

We therefore have the substantive hypothesis that forward short-term rates change on the basis of errors made in forecasting the current short-term rate,

$$_{t+n}r_{1t} - {}_{t+n}r_{1_{t-1}} = f(_tR_{1t} - {}_tr_{1_{t-1}})$$

or,

$$\Delta_{t+n}r_{1t} = g(E_t)$$

where E is the forecasting error $(_tR_{1t} - {}_tr_{1_{t-1}})$, the difference between the actual one-year rate and the one-year rate which had been expected to prevail. If we assume that the functional relationship is linear it may be expressed as

$$\Delta_{t+n}r_{1t} = a + bE_t$$

Because a long-term rate is an average of current and forward short-term rates we also have the substantive hypothesis that unanticipated changes in the long-term rate are also based on errors made in forecasting short-term rates,

$$_{t+n}R_{jt} - {}_{t+n}R_{j_{t-1}} = h(_tR_{1t} - {}_tr_{1_{t-1}})$$

or,

$$\Delta_{t+n}R_{jt} = k(E_t)$$

where $n = 0, 1, 2, 3, \ldots$ years and $j = 1, 2, \ldots$ years.

Note that the measured long-term rate of a given maturity can change even though current or forward short-term rates applicable to specific segments of the term to maturity remain the same. Such changes are anticipated ones according to the expectations hypothesis and reflect unchanged expectations. For example, consider a rate structure at time t

where $R_1 = 2\%$, $R_2 = 3\%$, and $R_3 = 4\%$. Assuming simple interest, forward rates are $_t r_{1t} = 2\%$, $_{t+1}r_{1t} = 4\%$, and $_{t+2}r_{1t} = 6\%$. R_2 is an average of $_t r_{1t}$ and $_{t+1}r_{1t}$.

Let one year pass with no change in forward short-term rates applicable to specific periods so that $_t r_{1t}$ will be eliminated and $_{t+1}r_{1_{t+1}} = {}_{t+1}r_{1t}$ and $_{t+2}r_{1_{t+1}} = {}_{t+2}r_{1t}$. The measured two-year rate is now an average of $_{t+1}r_{1_{t+1}}$ and $_{t+2}r_{1_{t+1}}$ and is approximately equal to 5 per cent. One of the forward rates at t has been realized and the other has remained the same so that the rise of the market two-year rate from its previous level is an anticipated one. Strictly speaking, my hypothesis applies only to deviations from this recorded difference, which is the unanticipated change in the long-term rate.

2.2. Tests of the Error-Learning Model

Changes in forward one-year rates classified by maturity are, in fact, highly correlated with the forecasting error for the fifty-four annual observations covering the 1901–1954 period. The regression equations and correlation coefficients are in Table 1. These calculations were restricted to eight futures rates applicable to progressively later years because of limitations of the Durand yield curve estimates, the source of the data.[3] Changes in long-term rates are also highly correlated with the unanticipated change in one-year rates; these relations will be discussed in detail later in this chapter.

There are four principal characteristics of the relations summarized in Table 1. First, the correlations between the first differences in the futures rates and the forecasting error are high and positive; all differ significantly from zero. Second, the correlation coefficient tends to vary inversely with the maturity of the dependent variable. Third, the regression coefficient and hence the sensitivity of forward rates to forecasting errors also tends to vary dependably and inversely with the maturity of the dependent variable. The regression equation is

$$\log b = .856 - .074n$$

where the values of b are the regression coefficients of the regressions in Table 1, and n is the number of years later than t to which the futures

---

[3]See Durand, *op. cit.* Note that annual estimates were made for 1 through 10 years to maturity at one-year-to-maturity intervals, and also for 12, 14, 15, 20, 25, 30, 40, and 50 years to maturity.

TABLE 1. RELATIONS BETWEEN CHANGES IN ONE-YEAR FUTURES INTEREST RATES
CLASSIFIED BY MATURITY AND UNANTICIPATED CHANGES IN SPOT MARKET
ONE-YEAR INTEREST RATES, ANNUAL FIGURES, 1901–1954

$$\Delta_{t+n}r_{1t} = a + bE_t$$

(units of percentage points)

n^*	Constant Term (and its standard error)	Regression Coefficient	Correlation Coefficient
1	.00 (.02)	.703	.952
2	.00 (.03)	.526	.867
3	−.01 (.04)	.403	.768
4	−.03 (.04)	.326	.682
5	−.02 (.04)	.277	.642
6	−.01 (.03)	.233	.625
7	−.02 (.03)	.239	.631
8	.01 (.03)	.208	.590

*Number of years later than t to which the futures rate is applicable.

rate is applicable. The correlation coefficient is −.968. The high correlation indicates that one can efficiently describe movements of the yield curve as a whole in terms of a family of rates each member of which is systematically related to the forecasting error and hence to each other. Fourth, none of the constant terms of the regression equations differs significantly from zero, a point of some importance for the discussion of risk aversion in Chap. 3.

Forward rates and the forecasting error also tend to move in the same direction. The synchronization of forward rates classified by maturity and the unanticipated change in the market one-year rate is summarized in Table 2.

Since unanticipated changes in marginal interest rates are highly correlated with the forecasting error, it must follow that unanticipated changes in the long-term rate, an average of the marginals, are also highly correlated with the forecasting error. Unfortunately, data limitations

TABLE 2. SYNCHRONIZATION OF ONE-YEAR FUTURES INTEREST RATES
CLASSIFIED BY MATURITY AND UNANTICIPATED CHANGES IN SPOT MARKET
ONE-YEAR INTEREST RATES, ANNUAL FIGURES, 1901–1954

A. When the Forecasting Error Was Positive (19 Years)

	Number of Years in the Future at Which Futures Rate is Applicable								Total
	1	2	3	4	5	6	7	8	
Increased	19	17	16	16	16	15	16	16	150
Unchanged	0	0	0	0	0	0	0	0	0
Decreased	0	2	3	3	3	4	3	3	21

B. When the Forecasting Error Was Negative (35 Years)

	Number of Years in the Future at Which Futures Rate is Applicable								Total
	1	2	3	4	5	6	7	8	
Increased	3	7	8	7	8	7	7	9	56
Unchanged	1	0	0	0	1	2	1	1	6
Decreased	31	28	27	28	26	26	27	25	253

preclude giving precise empirical content to this hypothesis. To measure the unanticipated change requires taking the difference between the actual change and the anticipated change. According to the expectations hypothesis, the anticipated change in a year in the yield of a bond of j years to maturity requires data of market yields of $j + 1$ as well as j years to maturity. However, Durand's basic yields at one-year intervals are not available beyond ten years to maturity.

If the actual change in a long-term rate is substituted as the dependent variable, some unavoidable errors are introduced into the calculations. The errors tend to be small ones which decline in importance as the maturity of the long-term rate lengthens. Consider, for example, a thirty-year rate in the regression

$$\Delta_t R_{30_t} = a + bE_t$$

the model tested below. Within the context of this model being tested, the correlation coefficient slightly overstates the strength of the relationship because a small component of the long rate has been correlated with itself. The estimating equation,

$$(_tR_{30_t} - _{t-1}R_{30_{t-1}}) = a + b\left[(1 + _tR_{1_t}) - \frac{(1 + _{t-1}R_{2_{t-1}})}{(1 + _{t-1}R_{1_{t-1}})}\right]$$

contains common elements on both sides of the equation. Consider that

$$\frac{(1 + _{t-1}R_{2_{t-1}})^2}{(1 + _{t-1}R_{1_{t-1}})} = (1 + _tr_{1_{t-1}})$$

where $_tr_{1_{t-1}}$, the forward one-year rate for period t given by the rate structure at $t - 1$, is a component of R_{30} because

$$(1 + _{t-1}R_{30_{t-1}}) = \sqrt[30]{(1 + _{t-1}R_{1_{t-1}})(1 + _tr_{1_{t-1}}) \ldots (1 + _{t+28}r_{1_{t-1}})}$$

Also, $_{t+1}R_{1_{t+1}}$ is a component of $_{t+1}R_{30_{t+1}}$ because

$$(1 + _tR_{30_t}) = \sqrt[30]{(1 + _tR_{1_t}) \ldots (1 + _{t+29}r_{1_t})}$$

The common element is very small, however, contributing to only one of 30 terms, the geometric mean of whose product is the dependent variable. This can be seen clearly with the help of the following example of an extreme case. Assume $_{t-1}R_{30_{t-1}} = 5\%$, and that all forward rates also are 5 per cent. Let one year pass and let us also assume that all forward rates remain unchanged but that the spot one-year rate rises to 10 per cent from the 5 per cent it had been the year before. Under these conditions R_{30} will rise from 5 per cent in period $t - 1$ to 5.16 per cent in period t, or approximately 1/30 of ΔR_1. The regression equation $\Delta R_{30} = .00 + .27\Delta R_1$ indicates clearly that ΔR_{30} relative to ΔR_1 is roughly nine times greater than this ratio so that ΔR_1 contributed little to the explanation of ΔR_{30}. The amount of spurious correlation introduced by correlating changes in the long-term rate with part of itself varies inversely with the maturity of the long-term rate in question. Note that of the 30 one-year rates which are the components of the thirty-year market rate, only 29 are common to successive thirty-year market rates in the annual series. R_1 is eliminated by the passing of time, and a new $_{t+29}r_{1_t}$ is added at the furthest end.

Changes in long-term rates are highly correlated with the forecasting error. As can easily be seen in Fig. 1 there are long secular swings of long-term rates, there the thirty-year rate, so that the series has a high degree of serial correlation. Nevertheless, virtually the identical regression results were obtained when the regression was calculated for the level

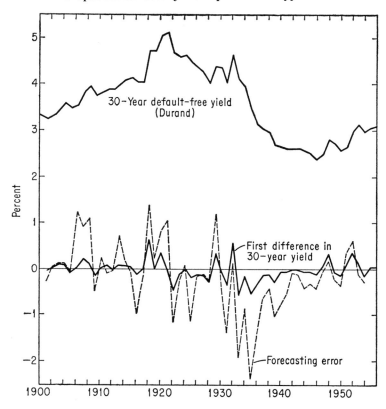

Fig. 1. Thirty-year default-free bond yields, changes in yields, and the forecasting error, annual figures, 1900–1954.

figures rather than the first differences. The multiple regression equation

$$_tR_{30_t} = .04 + .97\ _{t-1}R_{30_{t-1}} + .25E_t$$
$$\quad\ \ (.09)\qquad (.02)\qquad\qquad (.02)$$

The R^2 was .972.

Taking first differences of R_{30} as the dependent variable is equivalent to assigning a zero value to the constant term in the multiple regression and a value of unity to regression coefficient of $_{t-1}R_{30_{t-1}}$. The results of the multiple regression show that both the constant term and the regression coefficient are approximately but 1.5 standard errors from zero and one respectively. Thus, it is not unexpected that the regression coefficient of E_t and its standard error are the same in both the simple and the

TABLE 3. ACTUAL AND PREDICTED DURAND THIRTY-YEAR BASIC YIELDS, FORECASTING ERRORS, AND RESIDUALS, ANNUAL FIGURES, 1900–1954

	Durand Thirty-Year Basic Yield	Δ Col. 2	Durand One-Year Basic Yield	Expected One-Year Rate	Col. 4 − Col. 5 = *Error*	Predicted Col. 3 (= .03 + .25 Col. 6)	Residual: (Col. 3 − Col. 7)
1	2	3	4	5	6	7	8
1900	3.30		3.97				
01	3.25	−.05	3.25	3.53	−.28	−.04	−.01
02	3.30	.05	3.30	3.25	.05	.04	.01
03	3.45	.15	3.45	3.30	.15	.07	.08
04	3.60	.15	3.60	3.45	.15	.07	.08
1905	3.50	−.10	3.50	3.60	−.10	.00	−.10
06	3.55	.05	4.75	3.50	1.25	.34	−.29
07	3.80	.25	4.87	3.95	.92	.26	−.01
08	3.95	.15	5.10	3.99	1.11	.31	−.16
09	3.77	−.18	4.03	4.50	−.47	−.09	−.09
1910	3.80	.03	4.25	3.99	.26	.10	−.07
11	3.90	.10	4.09	4.17	−.08	.01	.09
12	3.90	.00	4.04	4.07	−.03	.02	−.02
13	4.00	.10	4.74	4.02	.72	.21	−.11
14	4.10	.10	4.64	4.44	.20	.08	.02
1915	4.15	.05	4.47	4.52	−.05	.02	.03
16	4.05	−.10	3.48	4.43	−.95	−.21	.11
17	4.05	.00	4.05	4.14	−.09	.01	−.01
18	4.75	.70	5.48	4.05	1.43	.39	.31
19	4.75	.00	5.58	5.34	.24	.09	−.09
1920	5.10	.35	6.11	5.28	.83	.24	.11
21	5.17	.07	6.94	5.87	1.07	.30	−.23
22	4.71	−.46	5.31	6.47	−1.15	−.26	−.20
23	4.61	−.10	5.01	5.25	−.24	−.03	−.07
24	4.66	.05	5.02	4.95	.07	.01	.04
1925	4.50	−.16	3.85	4.96	−1.11	−.25	.09
26	4.40	−.10	4.40	4.51	−.11	.00	−.10
27	4.30	−.10	4.30	4.40	−.10	.00	−.10
28	4.05	−.25	4.05	4.30	−.25	−.03	−.22
29	4.42	.37	5.27	4.05	1.22	.34	.03
1930	4.40	−.02	4.40	4.81	−.41	−.07	.05
31	4.10	−.30	3.05	4.40	−1.35	−.31	.01
32	4.70	.60	3.99	3.85	.14	.07	.53
33	4.15	−.55	2.60	4.49	−1.89	−.45	−.10
34	3.99	−.16	2.62	3.44	−.82	−.18	.02

TABLE 3 — *Continued*

1	Durand Thirty-Year Basic Yield	Δ Col. 2	Durand One-Year Basic Yield	Expected One-Year Rate	Col. 4 − Col. 5 = *Error*	Predicted Col. 3 (= .03 + .25 Col. 6)	Residual: (Col. 3 − Col. 7)
1	2	3	4	5	6	7	8
1935	3.50	−.49	1.05	3.38	−2.33	−.56	.07
36	3.20	−.30	.61	1.95	−1.34	−.31	.01
37	3.08	−.12	.69	1.31	−.62	−.13	.01
38	3.00	−.08	.85	1.29	−.44	−.08	.00
39	2.75	−.25	.57	1.57	−1.00	−.22	.03
1940	2.70	−.05	.41	1.15	−.74	−.16	.11
41	2.65	−.05	.41	.93	−.52	−.10	.05
42	2.65	.00	.81	.87	−.06	.01	−.01
43	2.65	.00	1.17	1.27	−.10	.00	.00
44	2.60	−.05	1.08	1.49	−.41	−.07	.02
1945	2.55	−.05	1.02	1.32	−.30	−.05	.00
46	2.43	−.12	.86	1.28	−.42	−.08	−.04
47	2.50	.07	1.05	1.08	−.03	.02	.05
48	2.80	.30	1.60	1.39	.21	.08	.22
49	2.74	−.06	1.60	1.82	−.22	−.03	−.03
1950	2.58	−.16	1.42	1.76	−.34	−.06	−.10
51	2.67	.09	2.05	1.66	.39	.13	−.04
52	3.00	.33	2.73	2.15	.58	.18	.15
53	3.15	.15	2.62	2.73	−.11	.00	.15
54	3.00	−.15	2.40	2.68	−.28	−.04	−.11

multiple correlations, or that the .82 value of the simple correlation coefficient $r\Delta_t R_{30_t} E_t$ is also equal to the value of the partial correlation coefficient.[4]

If the thirty-year basic yield is taken as the long-term rate, the regression equation is

$$\Delta_t R_{30_t} = .03 + 0.25 E_t$$
$$\quad\quad\;\; (.07) \quad\; (.02)$$

where units are also in percentage points. The correlation coefficient is +.82. The thirty-year basic yield, the first differences of the thirty-year

[4]Note that the hypothesis under examination asserts that the *level* of the forecasting error is associated with the *change* in long-term rates. It may also be misleading to present the correlation results for the level figures as a test of the hypothesis because of the serial correlation of R_{30}.

The values of the parameters a, c, and d are all less than 1.5 their respective standard errors and do not differ significantly from zero at the 15 per cent level. These results suggest that summing E_{t-1} and E_{t-2} and treating the sum as one variable would make the lagged errors statistically significant. The negative sign is rather puzzling and suggests some extrapolation of trend in the revision of expectations.

2.3. Implications of the Model and Suggestions for Further Research

What are some of the implications of these results? First, the futures market in loan funds reacts quickly to forecasting errors. Second, expectations are revised only on the basis of forecasting errors made within the same year the revisions take place. Previous errors have little, if any, effect on expectations. In other words, sunk errors are sunk.

It is important to note that observations have been taken once a year only. It may well be that using semi-annual, quarterly, or monthly observations to test the model will lead to modifications of these statements and also yield more precise information on the dynamics of the adaptive[6] mechanism upon which the model rests. Durand has published basic yields on a quarterly basis for the 1952–1957 period, and the *Treasury Bulletin* has presented a yield curve for marketable Treasury obligations on a monthly basis since February, 1939. Unfortunately, although Treasury yields are potentially the best source of data, there are serious problems involved in using these data for additional tests of the model. Some of the difficulties are listed in Appendix A. The Durand quarterly series may not provide additional data for further tests of the model because for most quarters he was unable to estimate reliable basic yields for maturities shorter than five years. Where these data are available, it is always for the first quarter of the year in question, the quarter on which the annual series is based.

2.4. Movements of the Yield Curve

This model is not a "bootstraps" theory of the term structure; it is definitely operational. The model asserts that expectations determine

---

[6]See H. A. Simon, "Theories of Decision-Making in Economics and Behavioral Science," *American Economic Review*, **49** (June, 1959), 271 for a more extensive discussion of adaptive, or learning models.

TABLE 3 — *Continued*

1	Durand Thirty-Year Basic Yield	Δ Col. 2	Durand One-Year Basic Yield	Expected One-Year Rate	Col. 4 − Col. 5 = Error	Predicted Col. 3 (= .03 + .25 Col. 6)	Residual: (Col. 3 − Col. 7)
1	2	3	4	5	6	7	8
1935	3.50	−.49	1.05	3.38	−2.33	−.56	.07
36	3.20	−.30	.61	1.95	−1.34	−.31	.01
37	3.08	−.12	.69	1.31	−.62	−.13	.01
38	3.00	−.08	.85	1.29	−.44	−.08	.00
39	2.75	−.25	.57	1.57	−1.00	−.22	.03
1940	2.70	−.05	.41	1.15	−.74	−.16	.11
41	2.65	−.05	.41	.93	−.52	−.10	.05
42	2.65	.00	.81	.87	−.06	.01	−.01
43	2.65	.00	1.17	1.27	−.10	.00	.00
44	2.60	−.05	1.08	1.49	−.41	−.07	.02
1945	2.55	−.05	1.02	1.32	−.30	−.05	.00
46	2.43	−.12	.86	1.28	−.42	−.08	−.04
47	2.50	.07	1.05	1.08	−.03	.02	.05
48	2.80	.30	1.60	1.39	.21	.08	.22
49	2.74	−.06	1.60	1.82	−.22	−.03	−.03
1950	2.58	−.16	1.42	1.76	−.34	−.06	−.10
51	2.67	.09	2.05	1.66	.39	.13	−.04
52	3.00	.33	2.73	2.15	.58	.18	.15
53	3.15	.15	2.62	2.73	−.11	.00	.15
54	3.00	−.15	2.40	2.68	−.28	−.04	−.11

multiple correlations, or that the .82 value of the simple correlation coefficient $r\Delta_t R_{30_t} E_t$ is also equal to the value of the partial correlation coefficient.[4]

If the thirty-year basic yield is taken as the long-term rate, the regression equation is

$$\Delta_t R_{30_t} = .03 + 0.25 E_t$$
$$\qquad\qquad (.07) \qquad (.02)$$

where units are also in percentage points. The correlation coefficient is +.82. The thirty-year basic yield, the first differences of the thirty-year

---

[4]Note that the hypothesis under examination asserts that the *level* of the forecasting error is associated with the *change* in long-term rates. It may also be misleading to present the correlation results for the level figures as a test of the hypothesis because of the serial correlation of R_{30}.

The values of the parameters a, c, and d are all less than 1.5 their respective standard errors and do not differ significantly from zero at the 15 per cent level. These results suggest that summing E_{t-1} and E_{t-2} and treating the sum as one variable would make the lagged errors statistically significant. The negative sign is rather puzzling and suggests some extrapolation of trend in the revision of expectations.

2.3. Implications of the Model and Suggestions for Further Research

What are some of the implications of these results? First, the futures market in loan funds reacts quickly to forecasting errors. Second, expectations are revised only on the basis of forecasting errors made within the same year the revisions take place. Previous errors have little, if any, effect on expectations. In other words, sunk errors are sunk.

It is important to note that observations have been taken once a year only. It may well be that using semi-annual, quarterly, or monthly observations to test the model will lead to modifications of these statements and also yield more precise information on the dynamics of the adaptive[6] mechanism upon which the model rests. Durand has published basic yields on a quarterly basis for the 1952–1957 period, and the *Treasury Bulletin* has presented a yield curve for marketable Treasury obligations on a monthly basis since February, 1939. Unfortunately, although Treasury yields are potentially the best source of data, there are serious problems involved in using these data for additional tests of the model. Some of the difficulties are listed in Appendix A. The Durand quarterly series may not provide additional data for further tests of the model because for most quarters he was unable to estimate reliable basic yields for maturities shorter than five years. Where these data are available, it is always for the first quarter of the year in question, the quarter on which the annual series is based.

2.4. Movements of the Yield Curve

This model is not a "bootstraps" theory of the term structure; it is definitely operational. The model asserts that expectations determine

---

[6]See H. A. Simon, "Theories of Decision-Making in Economics and Behavioral Science," *American Economic Review*, **49** (June, 1959), 271 for a more extensive discussion of adaptive, or learning models.

TABLE 3 — *Continued*

1	Durand Thirty-Year Basic Yield	Δ Col. 2	Durand One-Year Basic Yield	Expected One-Year Rate	Col. 4 − Col. 5 = Error	Predicted Col. 3 (= .03 + .25 Col. 6)	Residual: (Col. 3 − Col. 7)
1	2	3	4	5	6	7	8
1935	3.50	−.49	1.05	3.38	−2.33	−.56	.07
36	3.20	−.30	.61	1.95	−1.34	−.31	.01
37	3.08	−.12	.69	1.31	−.62	−.13	.01
38	3.00	−.08	.85	1.29	−.44	−.08	.00
39	2.75	−.25	.57	1.57	−1.00	−.22	.03
1940	2.70	−.05	.41	1.15	−.74	−.16	.11
41	2.65	−.05	.41	.93	−.52	−.10	.05
42	2.65	.00	.81	.87	−.06	.01	−.01
43	2.65	.00	1.17	1.27	−.10	.00	.00
44	2.60	−.05	1.08	1.49	−.41	−.07	.02
1945	2.55	−.05	1.02	1.32	−.30	−.05	.00
46	2.43	−.12	.86	1.28	−.42	−.08	−.04
47	2.50	.07	1.05	1.08	−.03	.02	.05
48	2.80	.30	1.60	1.39	.21	.08	.22
49	2.74	−.06	1.60	1.82	−.22	−.03	−.03
1950	2.58	−.16	1.42	1.76	−.34	−.06	−.10
51	2.67	.09	2.05	1.66	.39	.13	−.04
52	3.00	.33	2.73	2.15	.58	.18	.15
53	3.15	.15	2.62	2.73	−.11	.00	.15
54	3.00	−.15	2.40	2.68	−.28	−.04	−.11

multiple correlations, or that the .82 value of the simple correlation coefficient $r\Delta_t R_{30_t} E_t$ is also equal to the value of the partial correlation coefficient.[4]

If the thirty-year basic yield is taken as the long-term rate, the regression equation is

$$\Delta_t R_{30_t} = .03 + 0.25 E_t$$
$$\qquad\quad (.07) \qquad (.02)$$

where units are also in percentage points. The correlation coefficient is +.82. The thirty-year basic yield, the first differences of the thirty-year

[4]Note that the hypothesis under examination asserts that the *level* of the forecasting error is associated with the *change* in long-term rates. It may also be misleading to present the correlation results for the level figures as a test of the hypothesis because of the serial correlation of R_{30}.

yield, and the forecasting error are shown in Fig. 1 for the annual observations during the 1901–1954 period. Figure 2 shows the actual change in the thirty-year rate, the change in the thirty-year rate predicted by the regression, and the residuals. Note the apparent absence of serial correlation in the two regressed series and in the residuals. The data for these charts were taken from Table 3.

Changes in other long-term maturities are also highly correlated with the forecasting error. Table 4 contains the relations between selected long-term rates and the forecasting error. Note that the regression coefficient varies inversely with maturity. The inverse relationship is consistent with the behavior of forward rates as they become more distant.[5] Further, it is this empirical relationship which is responsible for the greater variability of shorter term rates summarized in Table 6. In addition, the correlation coefficient also varies inversely with the maturity of the dependent variable. This is so because of two factors: first, the inverse relationship between the correlation coefficient and the maturity of the marginal rates in the correlation between forward rates of different maturities and the forecasting error; and second, the inverse relationship

TABLE 4. RELATIONS BETWEEN CHANGES IN LONG-TERM DEFAULT-FREE INTEREST RATES OF SELECTED MATURITIES AND UNANTICIPATED CHANGES IN DEFAULT-FREE ONE-YEAR INTEREST RATES, ANNUAL FIGURES, 1901–1954

$$\Delta_t R_{jt} = a + bE_t$$

(units of percentage points)

Years to Maturity	a	b	Correlation Coefficient
5	.05	.48	.87
10	.04	.36	.84
15	.03	.30	.84
20	.03	.26	.83
25	.03	.26	.83
30	.03	.25	.82

between the weight of the spurious element in the correlation and the maturity of the dependent variable discussed previously.

The high degree of synchronization of the measured change in the long-term rate and the change in the long-term rate predicted from the

---

[5] See Table 1.

regression equation can be seen in Fig. 2 and Table 5. In the small number of cases in which the long-term rate did not move in the direction predicted from the regression equation, the amount of predicted change was small. For example, in the upper middle cell are four cases in which a rise in rates was predicted but rates remained unchanged. The predicted revisions were 0.02, 0.02, 0.09, and 0.01 of one per cent. In addition, deviations from perfect synchronization involved either no response of the long-term rate to a small predicted increase or relatively small shifts in the long-term rate when none was predicted from the regression equation. *In no case did bond yields rise when a decline was predicted, nor did they fall when a rise was predicted.*

TABLE 5. SIGN OF PREDICTED AND ACTUAL ΔR_{30}, ANNUAL OBSERVATIONS, 1901–1954

Predicted ΔR_{30}	Sign of Actual ΔR_{30}			
	+	0	−	Total
+	21	4	0	25
0	1	1	3	5
−	0	0	24	24
Total	22	5	27	54

If long-term rates are revised on the basis of unanticipated changes in short-term rates, then these revisions may be related to errors made in previous periods $t - 1, t - 2$, etc., as well as contemporaneous errors. In other words, expectations may be revised on the basis of some weighted average, or distributed lag, of errors in periods $t, t - 1, t - 2$, and so forth.

The results of the multiple regression

$$\Delta_t R_{30t} = a + bE_t + cE_{t-1} + dE_{t-2}$$

indicate clearly that E_{t-1} and E_{t-2} contribute almost nothing to the explanation of the change in the long rate in period t. The r^2 of the simple regression of $\Delta_t R_{30t}$ on E_t is 0.67. The multiple R^2 increases to only 0.70 when E_{t-1} and E_{t-2} are added as explanatory variables. The regression equation is

$$\Delta_t R_{30t} = .024 + .275E_t - .036E_{t-1} - .035E_{t-2}$$
$$\phantom{\Delta_t R_{30t} =} (.019) \quad (.026) \quad\quad (.027) \quad\quad (.026)$$

The values of the parameters a, c, and d are all less than 1.5 their respective standard errors and do not differ significantly from zero at the 15 per cent level. These results suggest that summing E_{t-1} and E_{t-2} and treating the sum as one variable would make the lagged errors statistically significant. The negative sign is rather puzzling and suggests some extrapolation of trend in the revision of expectations.

2.3. Implications of the Model and Suggestions for Further Research

What are some of the implications of these results? First, the futures market in loan funds reacts quickly to forecasting errors. Second, expectations are revised only on the basis of forecasting errors made within the same year the revisions take place. Previous errors have little, if any, effect on expectations. In other words, sunk errors are sunk.

It is important to note that observations have been taken once a year only. It may well be that using semi-annual, quarterly, or monthly observations to test the model will lead to modifications of these statements and also yield more precise information on the dynamics of the adaptive[6] mechanism upon which the model rests. Durand has published basic yields on a quarterly basis for the 1952–1957 period, and the *Treasury Bulletin* has presented a yield curve for marketable Treasury obligations on a monthly basis since February, 1939. Unfortunately, although Treasury yields are potentially the best source of data, there are serious problems involved in using these data for additional tests of the model. Some of the difficulties are listed in Appendix A. The Durand quarterly series may not provide additional data for further tests of the model because for most quarters he was unable to estimate reliable basic yields for maturities shorter than five years. Where these data are available, it is always for the first quarter of the year in question, the quarter on which the annual series is based.

2.4. Movements of the Yield Curve

This model is not a "bootstraps" theory of the term structure; it is definitely operational. The model asserts that expectations determine

---

[6]See H. A. Simon, "Theories of Decision-Making in Economics and Behavioral Science," *American Economic Review*, **49** (June, 1959), 271 for a more extensive discussion of adaptive, or learning models.

forward rates and that forward rates will change if, and only if, expectations also change. What is crucial in avoiding a "bootstraps" theory is that the model also gives empirical content to the process by which expectations are systematically altered. The structure can, of course, change through time even when expectations are constant because short-term rates are continuously being eliminated from the span of rates being averaged while other forward rates are being added. The contribution of this progression to movements of the structure as a whole when expectations are given is rather small.

Although the model asserts that forward rates change because of errors made in anticipating the short-term rate, it must be emphasized that the unanticipated change in the short-term rate is only the proximate cause of the revision of expectations. *The real but statistically unspecified independent variable is unanticipated changes in what the literature would typically call "the interest rate."* For given expectations, the entire brunt of an unanticipated change in "the interest rate" will be felt on the shortest end of the yield curve regardless of the source of the disturbance. Prices of long-term bonds cannot change much unless the disturbance alters expectations, even if the disturbance is financed completely by or associated with a change in long-term bonds outstanding. If the long-term rate were initially affected by an increase in bonds outstanding, speculation would force bond prices to return to their original positions. The speculation may take the form of borrowing in the short-term market to finance the purchase of the new bonds or selling short-term claims in order to acquire what appear to the speculator to be more profitable bonds. In this manner the short end of the yield curve will bear the bulk of the impact of the rise in rates. But, because short-term rates are now higher than had been anticipated, the market will revise upward expectations of future short-term rates, and the entire yield curve will tend to rise.

The same results will also follow if the unanticipated rise in "the interest rate" initially affected only short-term rates, for example, an increase in consumption expenditures financed by an increase in the demand for short-term consumer credit. Speculative shifts among maturities brought about by the new set of expectations will also tend to raise the entire structure. These factors will make the shape of a yield curve dominated by expectational elements largely independent of the maturity composition of the debt, a point which will be discussed in detail in Chapter 3.

This analysis is based on an interest rate disturbance that is superimposed on given expectations. If the unanticipated change in rates is associated with a change in expectations, then the mechanism would have to be modified to take both factors into account. For example, if interest rates were driven up by a disturbance associated with a war, and if the war was expected to be a short one, then the expectation should be recorded in the yield curve. In a free market the yield curve might approximate the "humped" yield curve the U.S. has experienced in recent years. Similarly, calculations of the forward rates implied by the "humped" yield curve observed during recent cyclical expansions may reveal market expectations of approximate business cycle turning points. However, the stable relationship between the change in the long rate and the forecasting error over the long fifty-four year period which covers such a wide variety of economic experience strongly suggests that the learning mechanism described above is the dominant factor in the revision of interest expectations.

The joint change in "the interest rate" and the revision of expectations of future rates cause synchronous movements of the entire yield curve, one aspect of which is that short-term and long-term rates tend to move in the same direction. The synchronization of forward rates was seen in Table 2. A similar synchronization of market rates classified by maturity is shown in Table 6.

Short-term rates are also more variable than long-term rates, not as a matter of arithmetic, but because of the empirical content of the market's adaptive behavior. Table 1 shows that the change in forward rates for a given forecasting error is inversely related to maturity. (It is interesting that the identical behavior in commodity futures markets has been established in a recent study.)[7] Similarly, there is a close and inverse relationship between the variability of market rates and term to maturity, for example, as reflected in the very high and negative correlation of (1)

---

[7]Joel Segall, "The Effect of Maturity on Price Fluctuations," *Journal of Business of the University of Chicago*, **29** (July, 1956). A more detailed treatment of the same problem can be found in his unpublished doctoral dissertation, "Differences in Price Fluctuations Arising from the Differences in Maturities of Contracts with Uncertain Returns" (University of Chicago, June, 1956).

TABLE 6. SYNCHRONIZATION OF INTEREST RATE CHANGES CLASSIFIED BY MATURITY, ANNUAL FIGURES, 1901–1954

A. When Majority of Measured Rates Increased (23 years)

Years to Maturity	1	2	3	4	5	6	7	8	9	10	12	14	15	20	25	30	40	Total
Number of times given rate																		
Increased	20	20	21	21	22	22	22	22	23	22	22	22	22	22	22	20	20	365
Unchanged	0	0	0	0	0	0	0	0	0	1	0	0	0	1	0	2	2	6
Decreased	3	3	2	2	1	1	1	1	0	0	1	1	1	0	1	1	1	20

B. When Majority of Measured Rates Decreased (29 years)

Years to Maturity	1	2	3	4	5	6	7	8	9	10	12	14	15	20	25	30	40	Total
Number of times given rate																		
Increased	4	3	1	0	0	1	1	1	1	1	1	2	2	1	1	1	1	22
Unchanged	2	0	0	0	0	0	0	0	0	0	1	0	0	0	1	2	3	9
Decreased	23	26	28	29	29	28	28	28	28	28	27	27	27	28	27	26	25	462

C. When Majority of Measured Rates Unchanged (2 years)

Years to Maturity	1	2	3	4	5	6	7	8	9	10	12	14	15	20	25	30	40	Total
Number of times given rate																		
Increased	2	2	2	2	1	0	0	0	0	0	0	0	0	1	1	1	1	13
Unchanged	0	0	0	0	1	2	2	2	2	2	2	2	2	1	1	1	1	21
Decreased	0	0	0	0	0	0	0	0	0	0	0	0	0	0	0	0	0	0

mean absolute changes in market interest rates classified by maturity; and (2) the number of years to maturity. The regression equation is

$$\log | \Delta \overline{R}_j | = .70 - .32 \log j$$

where j is term to maturity measured in years, and $| \Delta \overline{R}_j |$ is the mean year-to-year absolute change in rates of j years to maturity. The correlation coefficient is $-.99$.

Because all components of the yield curve tend to move together in a highly regular manner, one may view the shape of a yield curve at any point in time as the cumulation of previous movements of "the interest rate" and their attendant effects on expectations just summarized. This explains the tendency for short-term rates to be below long-term rates and for the yield curve to be an upward sloping one when the level of the yield curve is low, and the tendency for the opposite pattern of rates when interest rates are at historically high levels.[8] The systematic behavior of the yield curve is consistent with the view that all components of the term structure of interest rates are members of a family of rates which are related to each other by expectations and by similarly based systematic formation of those expectations. Also, the systematic behavior of the yield curve would appear to contradict the widely held view that the market for debt claims is "segmented" or "compartmentalized" by maturity[9] and that rates applicable to specific maturity segments can best be analyzed by rather traditional partial equilibrium supply and demand analysis where transactors act on the basis of preferences for specific maturities because of risk aversion and hedging considerations discussed above, or because of institutional restrictions.

The cyclical behavior of the Treasury yield curve during recent years is consistent with these general historical precedents. The Treasury yield curve was a sharply upward sloping one in the early phases of the 1954–1957 expansion when the level of rates was low. As the expansion progressed all rates tended to rise, but the shorter-term rates rose more than longer-term rates. By March, 1956, the yield curve was approximately horizontal beyond three years to maturity. A month later the level of the curve rose again and rates in the range of two to three years to maturity

---

[8]See figure, "Superimposed Basic Yield Curves, 1900–1942," on p. 17 of Durand, *op. cit.*

[9]For example, see John G. Gurley and Edward S. Shaw, *Money in a Theory of Finance* (Washington, D.C.: 1960), p. 117.

were higher than either shorter or longer maturities. This so-called "humped" yield curve was the typical one for the next eighteen months. During the entire period rates on the very shortest-term Treasury obligations were below the yields on the longest-term Treasury bond in the hands of the public.[10] The very shortest end of the yield curve was a sharply rising one during the later phase of the expansion, so much so that it was not uncommon to find securities in the three to six month to maturity range with higher rates than the longest term bond.[11]

The cyclical decline of the entire structure began in November 1957, three months after the business cycle peak had been reached in August. On October 31, 1957, the new issue of ninety-one day bills carried a rate of 3.60 per cent, the $3\frac{1}{2}$ per cent note due on May 15, 1960, was selling to yield 4.09 per cent if held to maturity, and the 3 per cent bond due in 1995 was yielding 3.60 per cent. Six months later, on April 30, 1958, which was in the neighborhood of the cyclical trough according to the National Bureau of Economic Research, ninety-one day bills were yielding 1.20 per cent, the $3\frac{1}{2}$ per cent note 1.68 per cent, and the 1995 bond 3.14 per cent. During the same period there was a marked change in the shape of the Treasury yield curve from the "humped" variety to an upward sloping one.

The "humped" yield curve returned during the ensuing business cycle expansion and its attendant rise in the entire yield curve. By December 31, 1959, ninety-one day bills were yielding 4.40 per cent, the 4 per cent certificate due May 15, 1960, yielded 5.03 per cent and the 3 per cent bonds of 1995 had risen to 4.10 per cent. The subsequent 1960 decline in rates followed the same general norms as all maturities fell, and short-term rates more so than long-term rates.

2.5. Comparison of the Error-Learning Model and a Naive Model

The fact that short- and long-term rates tend to have synchronous movements may lead some observers to present this fact as an alternative hypothesis to the one I have presented. An empirical regularity is not a

---

[10]This bond was the 3 per cent non-callable bond due in 1995.

[11]For example, on August 30, 1957, the 3 per cent bond of 1995 was selling at a yield of 3.60 per cent. On the same date, Certificates due on December 1, 1957, were yielding 3.61 per cent and Certificates maturing on February 14, 1958, were yielding 4.09 per cent. See *Treasury Bulletin* (October, 1957), pp. 40–43.

theory, and the regularity clearly cannot be cited as its own justification. In principle, there are an infinite number of hypotheses consistent with this, or any other, single empirical relationship. What is required to test an alternative hypothesis is that it be consistent with the observed regularity of short- and long-term rates moving together, and further, that the other implications of the hypothesis not be contradicted by still other data.

I have run several tests to try to distinguish between the error-learning model and this empirical generalization which may be viewed as a naive model. The error model is generally somewhat better in each individual test, but not significantly so. Part of the difficulty in distinguishing between the association of the change in the thirty-year rate and the forecasting error on the one hand, and the association of the change in the thirty-year rate and the change in the one-year rate on the other hand, is that the forecasting error and the change in the one-year basic yield are highly correlated and have an r^2 of .71. The regression equation is:

$$\Delta_t R_{1t} = .08 + .76 E_t$$

$r_{E_t \Delta_t R_{30t}}$ is higher than $r_{\Delta_t R_{1t} \Delta_t R_{30t}}$ but not significantly so. $r_{E_t \Delta_t R_{30t}}$ is $+.82$ and $r_{\Delta_t R_{1t} R_{30t}}$ is $+.78$. Using the Hotelling test for the significance of the difference between two correlation coefficients computed for the same population, I found that the two correlation coefficients were separated by a "Student's" t of but .28.[12]

I calculated a multiple regression with both E_t and $\Delta_t R_{1t}$ as the independent variables and with $\Delta_t R_{30t}$ as the dependent variable. The results of the multiple regression were:

$$\Delta_t R_{30t} = .02 + .167 E_t + .113 \Delta_t R_{1t}$$
$$\phantom{\Delta_t R_{30t} = .02 + }{\scriptstyle(.043)} {\scriptstyle(.048)}$$

where $R^2 = .705$, again giving no clear basis for choosing the error model. Both regression coefficients are significant, but the partial correlation coefficient $r_{E_t \Delta_t R_{30t} \cdot \Delta_t R_{1t}}$ is higher than the corresponding partial correlation coefficient $r_{\Delta_t R_{1t} R_{30t}}$. In addition, $r_{E_t \Delta_t R_{30t} \cdot \Delta_t R_{1t}}$ is .48 and $r_{\Delta_t R_{1t} \Delta_t R_{30t} \cdot E_t}$ is $+.31$.

---

[12]Harold Hotelling, "The Selection of Variates for Use in Prediction, with some Comments on the General Problem of Nuisance Parameters," *Annals of Mathematical Statistics,* **11** (1940).

TABLE 7. SIGNS OF $\Delta_t R_{30t}$ AND E_t, ANNUAL FIGURES, 1901–1954

ΔR_{30}

E	$+$	0	$-$	Total
$+$	18	1	0	19
0	0	0	0	0
$-$	4	4	27	35
Total	22	5	27	54

TABLE 8. SIGNS OF $\Delta_t R_{30t}$ AND $\Delta_t R_1$, ANNUAL FIGURES, 1901–1954

$\Delta_t R_{30t}$

$\Delta_t R_{1t}$	$+$	0	$-$	Total
$+$	18	4	4	26
0	0	0	2	2
$-$	4	1	21	26
Total	22	5	27	54

Movements of short and long rates are not as well synchronized as are the forecasting error and contemporaneous changes in the long rate. The synchronization of the original data is described in Tables 7 and 8. The relative synchronization of the two sets of series can be seen in Table 9. Here observations in the three cells along the diagonal in Tables 7 and 8, where the direction of the two series in question is the same, are designated "synchronous," and observations in the other six cells are designated "non-synchronous." The two proportions differ significantly at approximately the 5 per cent level[13] making the error model better in this test.

TABLE 9

	Error Model	$\Delta_t R_{30t}$ and $\Delta_t R_{1t}$
Synchronous	45	39
Non-synchronous	9	15

[13]The test for the difference between two sample proportions is described in W. Allen Wallis and Harry V. Roberts, *Statistics: A New Approach* (Glencoe: The Free Press, 1956), pp. 429–31.

2.6. Keynes and the Rate Structure

The mechanism I have described bears some resemblance to the one Keynes advanced in *The General Theory*. More so than in the *Treatise*,[14] he emphasized the importance of expectations in the determination of the long-term rate and asserted that central bank policy affects long-term rates, if affect them it does, primarily by altering expectations. This emphasis on the role of expectations is in agreement with the error-learning model. However, Keynes' judgment was not consistent with the evidence in several other respects. In the world of *The General Theory* expectations are deeply rooted in what Keynes called "convention" and "psychology" and he presumed that these behavioral characteristics tend to change slowly. He therefore held out little hope for a major revision of expectations and for a substantial fall in the long-term rate unless traditional central bank policies of operating either directly on the short end of the yield curve or through commercial banks were replaced by a new policy. Keynes suggested that the central bank operate on all maturities and deal in both public debt and high grade private bonds, and at the same time act to reassure the public that rates would be kept low. Lacking such reassurance, the public's expectations would be little affected and would tend to thwart central bank policy. In other words, Keynes would have held that the b coefficient is both highly variable and typically close to zero.

2.7. The Experience of the 1930's

The evidence, however, is that the long-term rate, rather than being sticky, fell sharply and continuously after 1932 (see Fig. 1). Never before in the recorded monetary history of the United States did riskless long-term rates fall so far so persistently in so short a period of time.[15] Similarly, never before in the recorded financial history of England did consol yields fall so far without serious interruption as they did from 1929 through

---

[14]Compare *The General Theory of Employment Interest and Money* (New York, 1936) pp. 202–4 with *A Treatise on Money, op. cit.*, pp. 353–73.

[15]See Macaulay, *op. cit.*, pp. 155 and 165, and Table 10, Col. 5, pp. A141–A161. Note that the sharp drop in yields Macaulay reported during 1862 and 1863 is a fictitious one because it reflected the rising premium on gold after the U.S. suspended specie payments. Yields on U.S. Treasury securities did not fall during the same period.

early 1935, the period in which *The General Theory* was written.[16] Rates may not have fallen enough to return the United States or England to full employment, but that is a separate problem. Whatever may be the deeper psychological roots of expectations, they were changed systematically over the entire 1900–1954 period under study and the evidence points rather clearly to the fact that the revision mechanism was a dependable one. In addition, the *b* coefficient for the long-term bond apparently is not close to zero; my estimate is 0.25.

The United States' experience after 1932 was completely consistent with this behavior. "The interest rate" declined every year after 1932, and although the market acted as if it expected future rates would rise, the market also anticipated rates which were substantially lower than they had been since the turn of the century. Over the same period the market never anticipated that rates would fall quite so much, or for that matter, for quite so long as they did. Each year actual short-term rates were lower than had been anticipated. Each year expectations were revised downward and the long rate fell.

There is also no clear evidence of a trend in the regression coefficient over the long period under study. The result of the multiple regression

$$\Delta_t R_{30t} = -.01 + .26 E_t + .00 T$$
$$\qquad\qquad (.03) \qquad (.00)$$

where T is time is consistent with no trend in the period as a whole. The multiple R^2 was .68. The simple r^2 of E_t and $\Delta_t R_{30t}$ was .67. In addition, when the long period was separated into two parts, one from 1901 through 1929, and the other for the remaining 1930–1954 period, the results of the two simple regression were:

1901–1929	$\Delta_t R_{30t} = .00 + .25 E_t$
	$\qquad\qquad\quad (.04)$
1930–1954	$\Delta_t R_{30t} = .10 + .31 E_t$
	$\qquad\qquad\quad (.04)$

---

[16]In January, 1929 the $2\frac{1}{2}$ per cent Consol was selling at $56\frac{3}{8}$. By January, 1935 the price had risen to $92\frac{19}{32}$. The only interruption to this price rise which drove yields from 4.43 per cent to 2.79 per cent was during the gold standard crisis of the last half of 1931. See A. H. Gibson, *Bank Rate, The Banker's Vade Mecum* (London, 1910), R. G. Hawtrey, *A Century of Bank Rate* (London: Longman, Green and Co., 1938), J. R. Hicks, *The Future of the Rate of Interest* (Manchester Statistical Society Papers; Manchester, England: Norbury Lockwood, 1958), III, especially the chart on p. 20 and Great Britain, Board of Trade, *Statistical Abstract of the United Kingdom* (London: His Majesty's Stationery Office, 1928–1940).

The r^2 for the 1901–1929 period was .65 and for the 1929–1954 period was .74. The two regression coefficients do not differ significantly from each other, although the b for the later period is higher. These results are consistent with still another simple regression for the 1934–1954 period

$$\Delta_t R_{30_t} = .06 + .27 E_t$$
$$\quad\quad\quad (.03)$$

when the r^2 was .81. Results for several other periods are presented in Table 10. I experimented with omitting 1932 from the regression because Durand reported that his estimates of the short end of the yield curve were much less reliable than usual. It is very striking that the regression results are virtually identical for the 1901–1931 and the 1933–1954 periods, which is further evidence of the absence of trend.

TABLE 10. RELATIONS BETWEEN CHANGES IN THE THIRTY-YEAR DEFAULT-FREE MARKET RATE OF INTEREST AND THE UNANTICIPATED CHANGE IN THE ONE-YEAR DEFAULT-FREE MARKET RATE OF INTEREST, ANNUAL FIGURES, SELECTED PERIODS, 1901–1954

$$\Delta_t R_{30_t} = a + b E_t$$

(units of percentage points)

Period	Constant Term (and its standard error)	Regression Coefficient (and its standard error)	Coefficient of Determination
1901–1954	.03 (.07)	.25 (.03)	.67
1901–1929	−.002 (.02)	.25 (.04)	.65
1930–1954	.10 (.03)	.31 (.03)	.74
1901–1931, 1933–1954	.02 (.02)	.25 (.02)	.74
1901–1931	.06 (.02)	.27 (.03)	.82
1934–1954	.06 (.02)	.27 (.03)	.81
1930–1931, 1933–1954	.06 (.03)	.28 (.02)	.86

In addition, Fig. 2 shows that there is no serial correlation or trend in the residuals, the presence of which might indicate a trend in the regression coefficient.

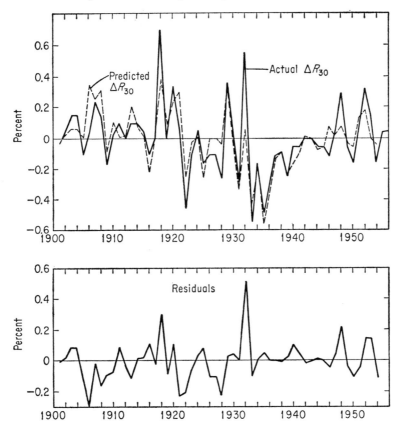

Fig. 2. Actual and predicted changes in thirty-year default-free
bond yields, annual figures, 1901–1954.

$$R_{30} = .03 + .25E$$

$$r = .82$$

There are several years in which the model predicts the direction of
change in the long rate but seriously underestimates the magnitude of
the change. Certainly other factors can influence expectations of future
interest rates and the disparities may have been caused by these other
factors. In fact, there would be much room for suspicion of the rather
simple and mechanical model I have presented if it always worked well.
Undoubtedly, an unanticipated change in interest rates is not the only

factor which can alter the structure. Other objective evidence presents itself; the market can learn from the events and recast expectations.

In 1918 the long rate rose much more than was predicted from the regression equation. The decline in bond prices for this observation in the first quarter of 1918 may have reflected expectations of a much longer period of war with its attendant rising prices and rising nominal interest rates than subsequently occurred. On the other hand, in 1921 and 1922 long-term rates fell more than was predicted by the model. These two residuals may be related to the return to "normalcy" and a more stable political and monetary setting, and to a sharp change in expected prices after the deflation of 1921. In the first quarter of 1932 the long rate was substantially higher than the model predicted. This may have been related to the general financial and economic chaos of the period, and possibly the prospect of the United States being forced off the gold standard. A simpler explanation is also possible. According to Durand, estimates of short-term basic yields in 1932 were not reliable.[17] It is not unlikely that the one-year rate was, in fact, substantially higher than was estimated, and that the unexplained component of the rise in the thirty-year rate was correspondingly smaller than has been indicated. Durand has also stated that there is more than usual likelihood of error in the shorter-term estimates for 1900 and for 1906–1908. Some of these years include relatively large unexplained variations in the long-term rate.

---

[17]Durand, *Basic Yields, op. cit.,* p. 17.

CHAPTER 3

Risk Aversion and the Yield Curve

I noted in Chap. 1 that the differences among the main alternative theories of the determination of the term structure of interest rates resulted from different presumptions regarding the existence or consequences of risk aversion in the futures market for loans. The expectations hypothesis asserts that risk aversion plays no essential role in the determination of default-free interest rates. Two other classes of hypotheses, however, do depend on risk aversion. This chapter will be devoted primarily to tests of these hypotheses. It will be shown that the evidence does not support them.

In one class of hypotheses, the Keynes-Hicks theory of normal backwardation is applied to the futures market in loans in much the same manner as it is applied to commodity futures markets. It shares the view with the expectations hypothesis that the market can best be analyzed as if speculators dominated; it differs from the expectations hypothesis in asserting that speculators have risk aversion, which leads to the forward rate being a biased estimate of the expected rate.

A second class of hypotheses asserts that risk aversion leads to hedging against interest rate fluctuations. Hedgers rather than speculators dominate the market, and hedging behavior is the basis for the borrowing and lending preferences of individual transactors and transactor groups. Interaction among them determines the relative prices of claims of different maturities, which is a hedging pressure theory applied to the loan market. The structure of interest rates in a hedger dominated market is related to the maturity structure of the debt. Because money is essentially a demand obligation, several implications of this class of hypotheses have interesting and testable implications for the demand for money.

3.1. Testing the Hicksian Model

As we have seen, Hicks asserts that a forward rate given by the market is higher than the expected rate by some risk or liquidity premium. Hicks contends that lenders are essentially speculators who have risk aversion. They require the payment of a risk premium to face uncertainty as holders of claims which fluctuate with movements of interest rates. Even accepting Hicks' own empirical presumption that risk aversion dominates the market, we have seen that risk aversion does not necessarily lead to a positive risk premium. But let us try to test the Hicksian model in his own version.

The Hicksian model can be expressed in the following terms:

$$1 + R_1 = 1 + r_1$$
$$(1 + R_2) = \sqrt[2]{(1 + r_1)(1 + r_2 + L_2)}$$
$$(1 + R_3) = \sqrt[3]{(1 + r_1)(1 + r_2 + L_2)(1 + r_3 + L_3)}$$

$$\cdot \qquad \cdot$$
$$\cdot \qquad \cdot$$
$$\cdot \qquad \cdot$$

$$(1 + R_n) = \sqrt[n]{(1 + r_1)(1 + r_2 + L_2) \ldots (1 + r_n + L_n)}$$

where $r_2, r_3, \ldots, r_n$ are expected one period interest rates in periods $2, 3, \ldots, n$, and $L_2, L_3, \ldots, L_n$ are the Hicksian liquidity premiums for periods $2, 3, \ldots, n$.

Forward short-term rates for periods $2, 3, \ldots, n$ will be $F_2, F_3, \ldots, F_n$ where

$$F_2 = r_2 + L_2$$
$$F_3 = r_3 + L_3$$

$$\cdot \qquad \cdot$$
$$\cdot \qquad \cdot$$
$$\cdot \qquad \cdot$$

$$F_n = r_n + L_n$$

Thus, if the expected rate is realized, the forward rate will be higher than the actual rate by the amount of the liquidity premium L_2, L_3, . . . , L_n. If, on the other hand, the forward rate predicts the actual rate precisely, it means that the actual rate is higher than the expected rate for the period, also by the amount of the liquidity premium. Under these conditions, the liquidity premium is a measure of the forecasting error.

It will be recalled that the expectations hypothesis asserts that the forward rates given by the market are unbiased estimates of expected rates so that the liquidity premium is zero. By contrast, the Hicksian model asserts that forward rates are biased estimates of expected rates. The magnitude of the bias depends on the values of the liquidity premiums L_2, L_3, . . . , L_n, all of which are greater than zero. Also, consistent with the assertion of the theory of normal backwardation that the yield curve is a rising one when rates are expected to remain unchanged is the requirement that $0 < L_2 < L_3 < \ldots < L_n$.

3.2. The Hicksian Liquidity Premium

The constant terms of the regression equations $\Delta_{t+n}r_{1t} = a + bE_t$ in Table 1 of the preceding chapter may be regarded as a reflection of the Hicksian liquidity premium. Consider $\Delta_{t+n}r_{1t}$ when $n = 8$. The regression equation $\Delta_{t+8}r_{1t} = .01 + .208E_t$ predicts that the forward rate will rise by .01 percentage points if E_t equals zero, that is, the actual one-year rate at time t is equal to the forward rate observed at time $t - 1$. Or, alternatively, the regression equation predicts no change in the forward rate applicable to period $t + 8$ when E_t equals approximately $-.05$. This suggests that (1) the forward one-year rate is typically greater than the expected one-year rate, (2) expectations are revised upward whenever spot one-year rates fall short of forward rates by less than .05 percentage points, and (3) expectations are revised downward when spot one-year rates fall short of forward rates by more than .05 percentage points.

For example, suppose the forward rate for a one-year loan beginning at year t measured at the beginning of year $t - 1$ is 2.00 per cent. The regression equation predicts that the forward rate applicable to year $t + 8$ will rise if the actual one-year rate is higher than 1.95 per cent, and will fall if the actual one-year rate is lower than 1.95 per cent.

Thus the .05 per cent difference may be a measure of the elusive risk or liquidity premium. However, the standard error of the constant term is .03 or triple its value of .01. Hence the constant term does not differ from zero. Similarly, the standard errors of the constant terms of the forward rates of other maturities are also larger than their respective constant terms, all of which are either zero or negative. This test does not, therefore, contradict the assumption of the expectations hypothesis that the risk premium on default-free claims is zero.

I find similar results if the same test is applied to a long-term rate, here the thirty-year rate. The constant term of the regression equation

$$\Delta_t R_{30_t} = .03 + .25E$$
$$(.07)$$

is smaller than its standard error and does not differ significantly from zero. If, however, the forecasting error is regressed on the change in the thirty-year rate,[1] the result is

$$E_t = -.129 + 2.67\Delta_t R_{30_t}$$
$$(.058) \quad (.257)$$

Solving for $\Delta_t R_{30_t}$,

$$\Delta_t R_{30_t} = .048 + .374E_t$$

The constant term, though small and close to zero, is again positive and more than twice its standard error.

The other regressions in Table 10 provide additional evidence. The most interesting feature of these regressions is the contrast between the constant terms for the periods before and after 1930. The constant term for the 1901–1929 period is essentially zero; the constant term for 1930–1954 is positive and triple its standard error.

The years which made the greatest contribution to the statistically significant positive value for the post-1929 period taken as a whole were

---

[1]There may be some point to presenting the error-learning model in this form rather than the running the regression as it was done initially because there may be larger errors of measurement of the forecasting error than there are of the Durand long-term rates. Bias introduced by the errors of measurement tends to be reduced if the errors affect only the dependent variable. The forecasting error is calculated from three observed short period market rates, and there are greater errors of measurement at the short end of the yield curve than at the longer end of the yield curve. This results from the greater relative spread between bid-and-ask prices expressed as yields to maturity, and also the greater fluctuation of the shorter-period rates during the three-month period, the lowest rates of which are included in the Durand calculations

1932 and 1933, the period of the greatest monetary and economic chaos. The change from no risk aversion prior to 1929 to a positive risk premium after 1929 is consistent with what appears to have been the post-1929 change in the temper of economic discussions and in the analytical assumptions of the economic literature.

This is a very weak test. More complex regression equations than these simple linear ones may be more appropriate, and the simple linear regressions may add an unknown bias to the constant term.

Several bits of evidence suggest that information regarding the existence of a positive risk premium can more readily be found in the markets for either Treasury obligations or other default-free claims with maturities of less than one year. During the 1900–1930 period, when a rising yield curve was observed in only two years, there were substantial periods of time when call rates were below essentially riskless bond yields (see Fig. 4). This suggests that very short-term rates may have some link to liquidity or risk aversion considerations, and that these considerations do not reach out to maturities as long as the one-year rate, the shortest in this analysis. It is entirely possible that a term structure similar to the "humped" yield curve of recent experience existed in these periods.

The comparison between Treasury yield curves and Durand basic yield curves is consistent with this evidence that default-free short-term rates are lower than are immediately apparent from the Durand data. It was noted above that the two yield curves tend to be parallel to each other beyond roughly three years to maturity, with Treasury yields somewhat below the Durand basic yields. The gap widens as maturities become shorter than three years. However, the difference may relate only to the greater marketability of shorter-term Treasury obligations.

Although liquidity considerations may have some minor influence on the yield curve, and possibly on the short end of the yield curve only, the evidence thus far contradicts the hypothesis that liquidity considerations are the primary factors determining the shape or the movements of the curve. In addition, for expectations of constant interest rates, a liquidity preference theory of interest along Keynesian lines would imply that yields are typically an increasing monotonic function of term to maturity. It is true that the typical yield curve in recent years has been of this shape, but during the thirty-year period running from 1900 to 1930 this rising yield curve was observed only twice.

3.3. Testing the Hedging Pressure Theory

The economic rationale for the link between hedging as a response to risk aversion and market preferences for securities of different maturities has already been developed. This section will examine the substantive content of the hedging pressure theory. The following section will be primarily devoted to a discussion of the apparent conflict between evidence of hedging behavior and the evidence supporting the expectations hypothesis, and a reconciliation of the two theories.

Hedging, and maturity preferences based on hedging, appear to pervade the market behavior of important transactors and transactor groups. For example, commercial banks with liabilities that are essentially payable on demand tend to hold the bulk of their earning assets in short-term claims. Purchases of housing tend to be financed by long-term mortgages, and acquisitions of less durable household capital such as automobiles tend to be financed by shorter-term loans, and so forth. Hedging behavior of this sort resulted in a close relationship between the ratio of short-term to long-term assets and the ratio of short-term to long-term liabilities of corporations in the fifty-seven non-financial industrial categories reported in the 1951 *Statistics of Income.* The regression equations are:

$$\log Y = 1.94 + 0.768 \log X$$
$$\log X = 0.54 + 0.983 \log Y$$

where Y is the ratio of short- to long-term liabilities and X is the ratio of short-term to long-term assets.[2] The correlation coefficient is .87.

In addition, few if any important transactors appear to be specialized to bearing interest rate uncertainty. A department store firm is specialized in buying and selling consumer goods, and not at all adept or efficient at trading in the futures market for loans. And, important financial institutions tend to operate so that they simultaneously incur liabilities and acquire assets of the same general maturity *on the average.*

---

[2]Short-term assets include the following: inventories, receivables, government securities, and various accrual items combined in the "other" assets category. All other assets were defined as long-term. Short-term debts are essentially the equivalent of the accounting concept of current liabilities. Long-term liabilities include debt having a maturity of more than one year, the dividing line between short- and long-term. Inventories of the tobacco manufacturing industry were shifted to the long-term asset class because the bulk of their inventories are ageing tobacco held for more than one year.

One important implication of a hedging pressure theory of the term structure is in direct conflict with a comparable implication of the expectations hypothesis. The expectations hypothesis implies that changes in the maturity composition of outstanding debt, when total debt is given, will have no long run effect on the term structure unless the changes in the supplies of or demands for securities of different maturities also affect either "the interest rate" or expectations of future rates. In the absence of the two sources of shifts in the term structure, the demand for securities of any given maturity will tend to have infinite elasticity, and the yield curve will be independent of the relative quantities of short- and long-term debt.[3] Thus, such financial operations as changes in either Treasury debt policy with respect to the maturity composition of the public debt or Federal Reserve policy with respect to the maturity composition of its portfolio will have no long run effect on the yield curve, unless the initial disturbance alters expectations of "the interest rate." Alternatively, in a market dominated by hedgers, a lengthening of the maturity of the public debt will raise long-term relative to short-term rates, a decline in inventories, short-term assets, will decrease the derived demand for short-term funds, thereby depressing short-term relative to long-term rates, and so forth.

The expectations hypothesis predicts movements of long-term rates when there is substantial variation in the maturity composition of outstanding debt. By contrast, during the 1917–1956 period, changes in maturity composition were unrelated to changes in the relationship between short- and long-term rates. The correlation coefficient of first

---

[3] An equivalent statement for the commodity futures market is that the supply of commitments is infinitely elastic. If the supply of commitments is infinitely elastic, then hedgers exert no influence on futures prices for given expectations held by the speculators. For example, given the expected price of spot wheat in December, the December futures price will not respond to a shift in hedgers' demands for commitments to deliver or to receive delivery of wheat in December. If, initially, a shift in hedgers' demands were to change the futures price, speculators would restore the price to its original position by supplying appropriate short or long commitments. For a systematic discussion of these points, see L. G. Telser, "Futures Trading and the Storage of Cotton and Wheat," *Journal of Political Economy*, **66** (June, 1958), and his unpublished doctoral dissertation, "The Supply of Stocks: Cotton and Wheat" (Department of Economics, University of Chicago, August, 1956). Part of Telser's study involved testing the hypothesis that the futures price equals the expected spot price in the markets for wheat and for cotton, which is the expectations hypothesis applied to the two commodity markets. He accepted the hypothesis that the two were equal, which is consistent with this form of the expectations hypothesis.

differences in the ratio of total short- to total long-term debt outstanding and first differences in the spread between short- and long-term
interest rates is but +.05. First differences were taken to eliminate
trend. The two series are correlated if the original data are used and
have a correlation coefficient of +.71.[4]

The same general relationships hold for the 1930–1956 period taken
separately. The correlation coefficient for the original data is +.82
but falls to .00 when first differences are taken.

I experimented with the possibility that changes in the spread
between short- and long-term rates lagged changes in the ratio of short-
to long-term debt. Lagging interest rates one year behind the debt
ratio did not change the results. The original data have a correlation
coefficient of +.45 but first differences again yielded a correlation
coefficient of .00 for the 1917–1956 period taken as a whole. Essentially
the same relationships were found when the lag relationship was reversed.
These results indicate that maturity composition, in itself, does not
determine the structure. However, it may well have an important
influence on the structure which is not immediately apparent from the
correlations, representing as it does the demand for funds side of the
market only. Both blades of the scissors are required. The introduction
of the supply side, where supply conditions are not dominated by expectational factors but by stable preferences for securities of different maturities, is needed to identify the influence of maturity composition.

It is by no means certain that maturity composition has had little
effect on the yield curve. But even if this were so, there presumably
would still exist some point beyond which shifts in maturity composition
would affect the term structure. If maturity composition has a negligible

---

[4]Interest rates are December averages of daily figures. The short-term rate is the
four to six month commercial paper rate. The long-term rate is taken from the
Macaulay series of adjusted high grade railroad bond yields (Macaulay, *op. cit.*,
Table 10, Col. 5), which was extrapolated beyond 1936 on the basis of the Durand
thirty-year basic yield and Moody's AAA bond yields. The Durand thirty-year basic
yield was taken as the February figure for the extrapolated series. Month-to-month
changes in the series were the sum of (1) month-to-month changes in the Moody's
AAA yields plus (2) an adjustment factor. The adjustment factor to compensate for
changes in the spread between the Durand thirty-year basic yield and the Moody's
AAA series was calculated by a linear interpolation of the year-to-year changes in the
spread.

The debt data were taken from several sources described in detail in Appendix B.

effect on the term structure, it means that for given expectations, the supply of speculative funds is infinitely elastic. There is, however, no reason to presume that infinite elasticity need hold over the entire possible range of variation in maturity composition. With larger shifts than have been observed thus far, or, for the analysis of shorter period movements in the structure, it may be necessary to take account of the interaction between speculators and hedgers.

Important reservations attach to these results for several reasons. First, the debt data for the private sector are subject to large errors of measurement. Second, the components of the data are not totaled consistently; for example, intercorporate debt is included but debt among households or unincorporated business is not. Third, it is not always clear how the data ought to be treated for purposes of testing the impact of maturity composition on market rates, principally because of problems of aggregation and consolidation.[5]

Even if the data were measured accurately and were treated consistently the problem of the appropriate level of consolidation of the private sector still exists, which precludes giving economic meaning to data which purport to measure total debt. Two commonly followed extremes are incorrect and are ruled out. In one, the private sector is treated on a completely consolidated basis. All debt among private transactors is netted out, and the net indebtedness of the private sector to the government remains. This treatment of the private debt is inappropriate for analyzing relationships among interest rates or the effect of maturity composition on the term structure. Given stable demand conditions, that is, conditions under which demanders of securities have stable preferences, the quantity of securities demanded is a function of (1) total assets, (2) expected returns, and (3) preferences. If the supply of securities (i.e., demand for loan funds) shifts, say, from the shorter to the longer portion of the maturity continuum, short-term rates will fall and long-term rates will rise. However, total private debt treated on a consolidated basis, net private indebtedness to the government, will remain the same and we cannot observe the maturity factors leading to or associated with the rate change.

At the other extreme, the private sector can be treated on a combined basis, and total private debt is then the sum of the debts of individual

---

[5]For a detailed discussion of these and related problems see Appendix B.

economic units. Again, total debt figures can be misleading. Given no change in rates or underlying conditions determining the structure in a market dominated by preference considerations, total debt will change with the degree of integration of the private economy. For example, let us say that households can finance the purchase of automobiles by borrowing either from banks or from finance companies which in turn borrow the funds from banks. If households shift from banks to finance companies as sources of consumer credit, total measured debt will rise but interest rates will remain the same.

Part of the difficulty in measuring and analyzing debt data for the market as a whole, and of identifying possible supply or demand schedules, follows from the fact that individual transactors are typically and simultaneously both suppliers and demanders in the same market. In addition, it is not unlikely that individual transactors and transactor groups shift between being net demanders and net suppliers. The market impact of any one transactor depends on his excess demand or supply of funds rather than the total quantities he demands or supplies. Under given conditions, where transactors are dominated by preference considerations, there is some rate at which net borrowings are zero. Net funds will be supplied at higher rates, and at lower rates net funds will be demanded. Both sides of the transactor's accounts must be measured to obtain these data.[6] To move from the individual to the market requires that the individual excess demand curves be summed. Market rates are determined where excess demands are zero. Whether sufficiently stable patterns exist to permit identification of these excess demand schedules remains to be seen.

3.4. A Reconciliation of the Expectations Hypothesis and the Hedging Pressure Theory

How can the cross-section data which support a hedging pressure theory of the determination of the yield curve be reconciled with the speculative behavior of the expectations hypothesis? In addition, since

---

[6]These data are available in the Federal Reserve Board's flow-of-funds system of accounts, although the long-term, short-term break is lacking or unsatisfactory for some transactor groups. Other problems may arise because the accounts are largely on a cash transactions rather than accrual basis. See Board of Governors of the Federal Reserve System, *Flow of Funds in the United States, 1939–1953* (Washington, 1955).

individual transactors do not tend to operate on all maturities, what is the market mechanism for propagating the systematic movements of the yield curve as a whole we have observed?

It seems to me that transactors face the wide range of possible uncertainties in the futures market for loans in much the same manner as uncertainty is faced in other markets. The existence of a wide range of choice does not mean that each transactor need cope with all the possible alternatives that are open to him. Rather, he can, and typically does, specialize in bearing some portion of the uncertainty. Thus, a commercial bank speculates in one section of the yield curve. It is the shortest end of the yield curve to be sure, but when a bank changes its investment policy to lengthen the typical maturity of its holdings from, let us say, four months to five months, it is effectively speculating on movements of future rates.

There appear to be a great many overlapping areas of the yield curve in which important transactors tend to specialize. At the shortest end are the commercial banks; somewhat longer are savings banks and savings and loan associations, and at the very longest end of the yield curve are life insurance companies. The market is given even more continuity by security dealers and professional short-period traders. In addition, there are also speculators who trade in commodity futures or the equity markets on a non-professional or non-specialized basis. Taken together, the transactors who specialize in coping with uncertainty in one part of the yield curve and act to reduce the variance of expected returns, plus others who need not have such preferences or restraints imposed by legal and institutional requirements, give the market a continuity that is not apparent from observing the narrow range of choice of any one large transactor group.

Thus, although banks do not shift between holding all short-term assets to holding all long-term bonds, and although insurance companies never dispose entirely of their bonds in order to shift into bills, the marginal shifts of these and other transactors are completely consistent with the observation that the yield curve as a whole tends to move in the same direction, and with a great deal of regularity of amplitude. These systematically related movements of the yield curve as a whole are not consistent with the notion that, because some transactors do not make substantial shifts in the maturity composition of their assets or liabilities, the market is a "segmented one."

Similarly, the fact that some transactors are not aware of the futures market in loans does not mean that the market cannot be analyzed "as if" they possessed such awareness. If speculators are sufficiently well financed, then the speculators will offset disturbances to the yield curve brought about by the hedgers. In other words, supplies or demands of ultimate borrowers and lenders cannot be aggregated in the usual Marshallian manner in order to arrive at some understanding of the formation of market prices of securities. Large and important transactors are both suppliers and demanders, and the Marshallian analysis is no more apt in this speculative market than it is in others.

3.5. The Yield Curve and the Demand for Money

The liquidity preference theory of interest implies a relationship between changes in the demand for money and changes in the spread between short- and long-term rates. According to the liquidity preference theory, relative rates of return on default-free securities are directly related to their proximity to money. In turn, proximity to money, or liquidity, is directly related to maturity. This implies that an increase in the demand for money proper will be associated with (1) an increase in the demand for money relative to other assets and (2) a corresponding increase in the illiquidity premium on long-term securities. The liquidity gap between money and bonds will widen as transactors attempt to move towards money along the continuum of liquidity.

If the liquidity preference theory of interest is correct, that is, if returns to securities arise because of their non-monetary qualities, and if these liquidity considerations alone dominate the determination of the yield curve, then we should find that fluctuations in income velocity are directly related to changes in the spread between short-term and long-term rates. When the demand for money increases (velocity falls), the short-term rate should fall relative to the long-term rate; and when there is a decline in the demand for money (velocity rises), the short-term rate should rise relative to the long-term rate.

However, there is little relationship between the level of income velocity and the spread between essentially riskless short-term and long-term rates for the eighty-seven annual observations covering the

1869–1956 period.[7] The correlation coefficient is +.40; for the first differences it is +.26. The call money rate was used as the short-term rate between 1869 and 1936; thereafter, the rate on three-month Treasury bills.

An alternative is to use the commercial paper rate as the short-term rate. This substitution yields an apparent relationship for the period 1895 to 1956. However, the apparent relationship is due entirely to the common trend in both series. It disappears when first differences in the two series are correlated. The correlation coefficient for the level figures is +.88, and for the first differences, +.12. In addition, there is a negative relationship between income velocity and the spread between commercial paper and the Macaulay series for the period between 1869–1895. This was a period of substantial and almost continuous decline in velocity. It was also a period in which there was no clear trend of call rates relative to long-term rates.[8]

This common trend in velocity and in the spread between short- and long-term rates since 1895 is responsible for the positive relationship between the two series which Selden has reported.[9] For the 1899–1919 period he correlated income velocity and the spread between commercial paper rates and the Macaulay series and found a correlation coefficient of +.09. For the 1919–1951 period he used Moody's bond yields as his long-term rate and found a correlation coefficient of +.77. For first

---

[7]Interest rates are annual averages of monthly figures. The short-term rate for the 1869–1936 period is the renewal rate on call loans on New York Stock Exchange collateral estimated by Macaulay, and the long-term rate for the same 1869–1936 period is the Macaulay series on high-grade railroad bonds taken from Macaulay, *op. cit.*, Table 10, Cols. 4 and 5, respectively. The character of the call loan and the call loan market changed substantially during the middle 1930's, and the rate on three-month Treasury bills has been used in its place since 1937. (See Appendix C for a description of the change in the short-term market.)

The long-term rate covering the period 1937–1956 is an extrapolation of the Macaulay series. The extrapolation procedure is described in footnote 4 of this chapter. The velocity data are from an unpublished National Bureau series estimated by Milton Friedman and Anna Schwartz. Money supply figures include currency outside the banks plus all commercial bank deposits adjusted for interbank and federal government deposits. Income corresponds to the Net National Product concept of Kuznets adjusted for war periods to a concept approximating the current Department of Commerce estimates of Net National Product.

[8]See Fig. 4 in Appendix C.

[9]Richard T. Selden, "Monetary Velocity in the United States," in Friedman, *op. cit.* See especially pp. 212–14 where Selden discussed his concept of the cost of money substitutes which is measured as the spread between short- and long-term rates.

differences of Selden's variables during the 1919–1951 period the relationship becomes a negative one and the correlation coefficient is −.44.

Although a change in the spread is not associated empirically with a
corresponding change in velocity, there may be another and somewhat
less direct link between a change in the maturity composition of the debt,
velocity, and the yield curve. Consider three sources of disturbance to
the yield curve in the liquidity preference analysis: first, an increase in
the supply of short-term claims, second, an equivalent decrease in the
supply of long-term bonds, and third, a fall in the demand for money
caused by an increased stock of short-term bills. If bills and bonds are
neither substitutes nor complements for money, then a change in the
maturity composition of outstanding debt will have no effect on the
yield curve or on velocity. First, an increase in the stock of bills, for
given expectations, will cause an unanticipated rise in the short-term
rate which will then affect the entire yield curve as expectations of
future interest rates are revised. Second, a decrease in bonds outstanding, for given initial expectations, will cause the entire yield curve
to decline. Taken together, the net effect will be zero.

If, however, it is true that short-term claims are substitutes for
money, then an increase in the supply of short-term Treasury obligations
will tend to cause velocity to increase. Both the level and the structure
of rates will depend on the involved and analytically uncertain chain of
events between a velocity change and a shift in the interest rate. The
error-revision mechanism will come into play if there is a disturbance to
the interest rate. That is, if an increase in the supply of bills decreases
the quantity of money the public wishes to hold, and if the public then
attempts to exchange the excess money for securities, the level of interest
rates will fall. To the extent that the fall is an unanticipated one, the
entire yield curve will decline through the familiar error-revision
mechanism, and short-term rates will decline more than long-term rates.
This result follows despite the fact that there has been an increase in
the quantity of short-term debt held by the public. If the level of interest
rates is in temporary equilibrium at this stage of the disturbance, and
if in moving to a long-run equilibrium the level of interest rates rises,
then the same mechanism will operate but with opposite sign. In the
long run, the structure of rates will tend to be the same, except as the
disturbance has changed either (1) the level of interest rates, (2) expectations of future rates, and possibly (3) the risk premium, if one

there is. At the same time, velocity as is typically measured — the ratio of income to the stock of money — will rise.

3.6. Implications of the Expectations Hypothesis for the Supply of Liquidity

Let us return to the implication of the expectations hypothesis that market excess demand schedules of securities of given maturities tend to be infinitely elastic at rates consistent with current and expected short-term rates. Of course, it is not necessary that all transactors have infinitely elastic schedules in order that the market schedules be infinitely elastic. It is only necessary that one class of adequately financed transactors have an infinitely elastic excess demand schedule. As in the case of the market dominated by speculators discussed earlier or a price leader in an analogous market context, speculators with given expectations adjust quantities of securities taken from or supplied to the market in order to maintain the structure of rates consistent with expectations.[10] Similarly, it would seem that financial intermediaries can produce whatever maturity composition asset holders prefer without significantly influencing the term structure of interest rates. Thus, it is not necessary that both the borrowing and the lending sides of the market have infinitely elastic market schedules in order to observe the market phenomena consistent with the expectations hypothesis.

There appears to be some confusion on this point, possibly because supply conditions tend to be overlooked in the analysis of financial markets. For example, consider the familiar proposition that begins with the assertion that holders of short-term claims essentially view them as composite commodities, part debt and yielding explicit pecuniary returns, part money and yielding implicit liquidity services. If so, holders of claims (lenders) can be in equilibrium when market long-term rates are higher than averages of expected short-term rates because the liquidity component must be added to the expected pecuniary returns.

If net lenders are in equilibrium when forward rates are higher than expected rates, net borrowers with the same expectations would not be in

---

[10]Note that a class of speculators may have infinitely elastic excess demand schedules when individual members of the class do not. The situation is analogous to a constant cost industry.

equilibrium unless there is a stream of illiquidity costs to them which exactly match the corresponding stream of liquidity returns to lenders. Borrowers' illiquidity costs are excluded by the considerations of the expectations hypothesis that imply the infinitely elastic excess demand schedules just discussed. Therefore, if liquidity returns to lenders are positive, averages of expected short-term rates to borrowers would be lower than the market long-term rates spanning the same periods. Suppliers of securities (borrowers) would be induced to shift out of long-term into short-term sources of funds until expectations and market yields ,are consistent. Short-term rates rise during the process as the quantities of short-term claims increase. Lenders' marginal liquidity returns correspondingly decline as they hold relatively more short-term debt. Abstracting from transactions costs, marginal liquidity returns tend to be driven to zero if the adjustments between expectations and market rates are complete in the sense that each long-term rate is an average of expected short-term rates. Under these assumptions, therefore, the liquidity or "moneyness" component of short-term or other non-demand obligations has essentially zero marginal content in equilibrium.

Note, however, that the maturity continuum in this analysis does not extend to demand obligations, debts which are typically employed as money. Private profit seeking transactors can generally issue desired quantities of obligations of any other maturity without institutionally imposed limits. By contrast, the stock of demand obligations is limited by well-known institutional factors. If reserve requirements and other restraints on deposit creation were eliminated, private transactors would increase the stock of demand obligations up to the point where the value of a unit of money equals its private marginal cost. Abstracting from transactions costs, as above, the value of each unit of money would also approach zero.[11] If the stock of money is composed of demand obligations only, the price level would tend to be infinite and presumably demand obligations would eventually be replaced by some other medium of exchange.

---

[11]Transactions costs and other private productions costs per unit of demand obligations would appear to be low in the real world, so that the value of money in this variant of a commodity standard will correspondingly tend to be low. This analysis suggests that transactions costs may play an important role in these and related problems because they appear to modify the infinite elasticity implications of the expectations hypothesis. A more detailed and potentially more useful analysis should include considerations of transactions costs.

It is this difference in supply conditions separating money from other claims which may appear to be close substitutes for money. This point cannot be overemphasized, especially in view of recent controversies in monetary theory and policy which have been provoked by arguments that money is but the starting point of a continuum of assets yielding a corresponding continuum of liquidity services, and that banks are but one among many institutions creating liquid assets. It appears that the typical discussion in this area abstracts from this crucial difference in supply conditions, and further, is also implicitly framed in terms of average liquidity returns to holders of claims, not marginal ones.[12] Even if supply adjustments are not complete, and transactions costs or market imperfections are, in fact, greater than assumed by this brief analysis, it would seem that non-bank intermediaries are relatively less important suppliers of liquidity at the margin that is often currently asserted. The stock of short-term claims may yield some average liquidity return, but there is no reason to presume that average considerations have special content in the analysis of financial markets not shared with the analysis of other markets.

Thus, the expectations hypothesis suggests that the implications for money income, prices, interest rates, and the like, of an increase in the quantity of deposits are not analytically equivalent to a corresponding increase in the quantity of Treasury bills or similar "liquid" instruments. The effects of an increase in the volume of deposits by the banking system to finance the purchase of long-term bonds are not the same as a corresponding increase in the volume of short-term claims issued by other transactors to finance the acquisition of similar bonds. It is clear that an increase in the stock of deposits increases the total "liquidity" of the economy. It is by no means clear that a change in the quantity of other "liquid" assets has the same consequences.

3.7. Summary and Conclusions

This study has explored the market determination of the term to maturity structure of interest rates. Following the suggestion of J. R. Hicks, the market was analyzed as a futures market in loan funds

---

[12]For example, see John G. Gurley, *Liquidity and Financial Institutions in the Postwar Economy*, U.S. Congress, Joint Economic Committee, Washington, 1960.

analogous to commodity futures markets, and a method for deriving forward or futures rates implicit in observed market rates was presented. The economic bases for speculation, hedging, and arbitrage in this futures market were examined. On a formal level, it was found that differences among principal extant hypotheses of the determination of the term structure were primarily related to different presumptions regarding behavior with respect to risk. Three classes of hypotheses were examined. First, that speculators indifferent to risk dominate the market so that forward rates given by the market are unbiased estimates of expected rates, making long-term default-free rates averages of expected short-term default-free rates. Second, that speculators with risk aversion dominate so that forward rates also include a risk premium, which is the Hicks-Keynes theory of normal backwardation applied to the loan market. Third, that hedging leads to borrower and lender preferences for short- and long-term funds and that relative rates are determined by net hedging pressures.

The need for independent evidence of interest expectations, the previous barrier to the empirical examination of the role of expectations, was eliminated by applying to the formation of interest rate expectations a variant of a simple learning model successfully applied to a wide range of economic phenomena. The model asserts that expectations are revised whenever previously held expectations are in error. Year-to-year movements of components of the yield curve and its implied forward rates during the 1900–1954 period were, in fact, systematically related to the difference between futures and realized short-term rates, and hence to each other. The systematic covariation of segments of the yield curve contradicts the widely held view that the market is a "segmented" one.

The evidence is consistent with the thesis that neither risk aversion nor risk preference play important roles in the formation of forward rates and that forward rates are unbiased estimates of expected rates. This confirms the theory that a long-term default-free rate of interest is an average of expected short-term default-free rates. In combination with still other evidence, the results contradict the Hicks-Keynes theory of normal backwardation, and although it was found that many individual transactors hedge against interest rate fluctuations, aggregative data fail to support a hedging pressure theory. The evidence also contradicts implications for the term structure of the liquidity preference theory of interest.

The data for this study were typically on an annual basis and a one-year rate of interest was generally the shortest maturity studied. Observations taken at shorter intervals may temper some of these conclusions, and a detailed examination of shorter maturities may lend some support to currently rejected hypotheses.

APPENDIX A

Measuring the Term Structure:
The Yield Curve

Yield curves for the best grade corporate bonds have been estimated by David Durand on an annual basis since 1900, and on a quarterly basis for the 1952–1957 period. Durand's presumption was that the highest grade corporate bonds are virtually free of default risk and that their yields are therefore a close approximation of default-free yields. The estimating procedure is described in detail in David Durand, *Basic Yields of Corporate Bonds*, 1900–1942 (*op. cit.*, p. 4). Subsequent annual estimates appeared in David Durand and Willis J. Winn, *Basic Yields of Bonds*, 1926–1947: *Their Measurement and Pattern* (*op. cit.*, p. 4), and the *Economic Almanac* (*op. cit.*, p. 4). The quarterly estimates first appeared in David Durand, "A Quarterly Series of Corporate Basic Yields, 1952–1957, and Some Attendant Reservations" (*op. cit.*, p. 4).

Briefly, the Durand annual yield curves were derived from averages of high and low sale prices of the best-grade corporate bonds during each of the months of the first quarter of the year. The prices were converted to yields to maturity by the use of bond tables. The yields were then plotted on scatter diagrams with term to maturity on the horizontal axis and yield on the vertical axis. A free hand trend line was drawn as an envelope of the lower limit of the observed points. The lowest yield for each maturity was examined to insure that spurious elements were not contained in the yield. The lowest yield is then an estimate of the riskless, or basic, yield. Yields for 1942 are based on January and February prices, and yields for 1951 and later years are based on February prices. For the quarterly estimates the central month for each quarter was used.

Yield curves for U.S. Treasury obligations have been estimated by the Treasury Department each month since February, 1939, and are published monthly in the *Treasury Bulletin*. Free hand curves, also fitted to rates derived from market prices, appear to have been drawn with less care and possibly less precision than the Durand series. Unlike the Durand series, rates have not been read off the curves for presentation in more convenient tables.

It is not possible to use federal obligation yield data for most of the period after 1900 when the Durand estimates are available for corporate bonds. There are several reasons for this. First, all federal obligations contained some element of tax exemption before 1940. Second, the market for federal obligations was a very thin one before 1917. For much of the period before the large increase in the public debt during World War I, the bulk of the outstanding U.S. bonds were held by national banks as cover for national bank notes, an institutional arrangement which tended to depress Treasury yields relative to others. Third, there were large gaps in the maturity continuum of the outstanding federal debt. Fourth, in more recent years there has been a problem of measuring the exact maturity of much of the debt because of the call option attached to many issues, a problem also shared by many corporate issues. Fifth, obligations nearing maturity often had spurious yields reflecting the market value of exchange privileges.

There are several further problems in measuring default-free interest rates beyond the maturity-duration problem discussed in Chap. 1. When estimating default-free interest rates from the market prices of securities with some default risk, one is never certain that the default element has been eliminated, or for that matter, that the error is a stable one. The Durand method eliminates the bulk of the default risk, but the fact that the yield curves based on the highest grade corporate bonds tend to lie above similar curves based on the yields of Treasury bonds is some indication that some default risk remains in the Durand estimates. The yield curves for U.S. Treasury obligations have been roughly parallel but somewhat below the Durand corporate yield curves with the possible exception of the very shortest maturities. In this area, the excess of the best-grade corporate over Treasury yields appears to widen. See basic charts following page 24 in Durand (*op. cit.*, p. 4) and Durand and Winn (*op. cit.*, p. 4).

Fitting a curve to a set of widely scattered observations whose boundary is uncertain may lead to an excessive smoothing of the data. The final smoothed curve may reflect, in part, the shape of the French curve used by the statistician. These practical problems of measurement are further complicated by capital gains being subject to a lower tax rate than ordinary income, and the fact that coupon receipts are typically taxed as ordinary income but the terminal payment of the face amount of the bond is treated as a tax-free redemption of capital.

Finally, there are the statistical and analytical problems posed by transactions costs and the spreads between bid and asked prices and yields. This study has explicitly neglected transactions costs. The spreads between bid and asked yields vary inversely with maturity, and spreads of corporate securities tend to be substantially wider than spreads of corresponding Treasury obligations, reflecting the typically thinner market for private debts. Many problems clearly require that yields be measured net of all transactions costs, not as means of bid and of asked yields as is usually done, but a detailed analysis of the role of transactions costs in the measurement and analysis of the yield curve is beyond the scope of this study.

Problems in the Measurement of Aggregate Short- and Long-Term Debt

The debt data for this study were taken from several sources. Estimates of private debt and state and local government debt were taken from the Department of Commerce series which appear annually in the *Survey of Current Business*,[1] for example, page 14 of the October, 1954 issue. Not all private debt outstanding is aggregated but is measured as the sum of all classes of legal indebtedness except (1) bank deposit liabilities, (2) the value of outstanding policies and annuities of life insurance carriers, (3) short-term debts among individuals and unincorporated nonfinancial business firms, and (4) the nominal debt of corporations, such as bonds which are authorized but unissued, or outstanding but reacquired.

Net rather than gross debt for the state and local and private sectors was used. State and local net debt eliminates state and local government holdings of state and local debt, and corporate net debt is that owed to all other entities, including corporations except to other corporate members of an affiliated system. All state and local debt was assumed to be long-term.

---

[1]U.S. Department of Commerce, *Survey of Current Business* (Washington: Government Printing Office, 1954).

Net private short-term debt was estimated as the sum of (1) corporate notes and accounts payable and (2) individual and non-corporate non-mortgage debt. The federal debt includes marketable direct and guaranteed federal obligations in the hands of the public, excluding federal debt held by government agencies, trust funds, and Federal Reserve banks. The dividing line between long-term and short-term federal obligations is a current maturity of one year. All data for the 1942–1956 period were taken from the *Treasury Bulletin*. For earlier years, figures on total marketable federal obligations were taken from *Banking and Monetary Statistics*. Adjustments to eliminate issues held by federal agencies and trust funds, and Federal Reserve banks were based on *Banking and Monetary Statistics* (pp. 330–33), Raymond Goldsmith, *A Study of Saving*, Table F-23, *Annual Reports* of the Board of Governors of the Federal Reserve System, and the Treasury Department release, "Statement of the Public Debt." The same sources were also used to divide the federal debt in the hands of the public between short-term and long-term by current maturity of one year.

The debt data have been broken down into short-term and long-term debt on a very rough basis, and there undoubtedly is substantial error in the allocation. The boundary line between short-term and long-term is typically taken to be one year to maturity. For present purposes, term to maturity should be measured on a current rather than original maturity basis. Corporate debt is reported on a current maturity basis until 1937. Thereafter, the data are on an original maturity basis. Some state and local government debt has a current maturity of less than one year as does some mortgage debt, but both have been allocated to long-term debt. Also, some private non-corporate non-mortgage debt has a current maturity of more than one year but the entire total has been allocated to short-term debt.

There is also the additional problem created by the use of the short-term, long-term dichotomy to classify rates and debt for the analysis of the term structure. The term structure is a family of rates, and one short-term rate and one long-term rate are but two among many members of that family. The quantities of debt corresponding to the prices given by the term structure clearly fall into more than two maturity classes.

Debts among members of the non-corporate private sector, that is, among individual households and non-corporate businesses, have not been included in the tabulation of total debt. On the other hand, inter-corporate debt has been included. Thus, shifts in financing patterns between the corporate and non-corporate components of the private sector will change the figures for total measured debt when, in fact, these totals have not changed.

Ideally, all debt data should be recorded on an accrual rather than cash transactions basis for this analysis. The original components of the debt data are not treated consistently with respect to these alternative accounting bases. Some components are recorded on a transactions basis, for example, the net indebtedness of governmental units, but other components such as corporate book accounts and tax liabilities are recorded on an accrual basis. At the same time, the book account items and the tax liabilities of non-corporate transactors are not accounted for at all. The item, Corporate "Other short-term debt," which is composed almost entirely of the tax liability account, was not included in the debt calculation although it is a component of the Department of Commerce estimates of corporate debt outstanding. This was done to treat the debt components on a more nearly consistent basis, because data on tax liabilities of individuals, short-term debt, are unavailable.

APPENDIX C

Secular Relationships between
U.S. Short- and Long-Term Rates

There is a very striking and frequently copied chart on short- and long-term interest rates in the periodically issued historical supplement to the Federal Reserve Board publication, *Federal Reserve Chart Book on Financial and Business Statistics*,[1] which appears to indicate that short-term rates were above long-term rates almost continuously from 1865 to the middle 1920's, and that the reverse has typically been the case since that time. The interest rates that are charted for the 1865–1936 period are the Macaulay estimates of four-to-six month prime commercial paper rates and his high grade railroad bond yields. (See Fig. 3, taken from page 37 of the September, 1958 issue of the chart book.) These comparisons are misleading and can easily give one the erroneous impression that the 1920's represented a watershed in the history of the relationship between short- and long-term rates of interest, that short-term rates tended to be above long-term rates before the 1920's and below long-term rates since.

Commercial paper rates formerly included both high transactions costs and more than nominal default risk premiums, and are therefore inappropriate for comparison with essentially default-free long-term

---

[1]For example, U.S. Board of Governors of the Federal Reserve System, *Federal Reserve Chart Book on Financial and Business Statistics, Historical Supplement* (Washington: U.S. Government Printing Office, Sept., 1958), p. 37.

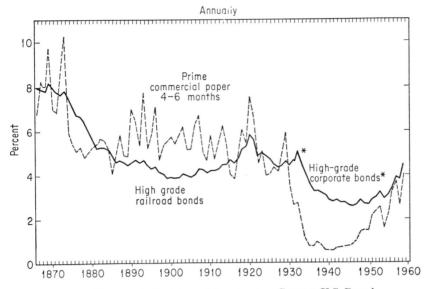

Fig. 3. Long- and short-term interest rates. Source: U.S. Board of Governors of the Federal Reserve System, *Federal Reserve Chart Book on Financial and Business Conditions* (Sept., 1958), p. 37.

yields. Commercial paper has not been a homogeneous financial instrument over the long period since commercial paper first became important just after the Civil War. In recent years the commercial paper market has been dominated by the almost completely default-free paper issued in large pieces by large sales finance companies.[2] By contrast, commercial paper in earlier periods was typically issued in small pieces by less well known names, had more than nominal default risk and experience, and was also sold in small lots.[3]

These facts were clearly recognized by the market and for the period between the Civil War and World War I commercial paper rates were typically one and one half to two percentage points higher than call money rates (see Fig. 4). The gap narrowed, and possibly was even

---

[2]See Donald P. Jacobs, "Sources and Costs of Funds of Large Sales Finance Companies," in the National Bureau Conference volume, *The Problem of Consumer Credit Regulation* (Washington: U.S. Government Printing Office, 1957).

[3]See Margaret G. Myers, *The New York Money Market*, Vol. I: *Origins and Development* (New York: Columbia University Press, 1931), pp. 315-37, and Macaulay, *op. cit.*, pp. A335-A351.

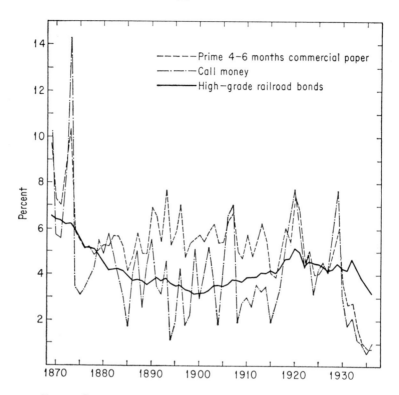

Fig. 4. Interest rates on call loans, prime four-to-six months commercial paper, and high grade railroad bonds, annual figures, 1869–1936. Source: F. R. Macaulay, *The Movements of Interest Rates, Bond Yields, and Stock Prices in the United States since 1856* (New York: National Bureau of Economic Research, Inc., 1938), Table 10.

virtually eliminated around 1920 as the default risk and administrative costs declined. In addition, the Federal Reserve Act made commercial paper eligible for rediscount at Federal Reserve Banks which may have tended to lower the commercial paper rate relative to other short-term rates.

If call money rather than commercial paper rates are compared with the high grade bond yields for the same period, we do not find any long period in which very short-term rates were above bond yields (Fig. 4). Rather, before 1930 call money rates tended to fluctuate around long-term rates, and with no clear-cut trend in the relationship between the two series.

The quoted rate on call loans cannot be used for these comparisons for recent years and for many other purposes because the character of the call loan and the call loan market have changed since the 1930's. Unlike earlier periods, the large New York money market banks are now prohibited by the Securities Exchange Act of 1934 from making call loans on the account of "others," that is, they cannot act as intermediaries in placing call money in the New York Stock Exchange. In addition, the prohibition of interest payments on demand deposits precludes their borrowing at call for relending to the stock exchange. Formerly, the rate was posted daily at the Stock Exchange Money Desk with a view to clearing the market for call loans.

The Money Desk has been closed for some years, and the call loan rate is posted by the large New York banks and is the rate on loans to brokers on stock exchange collateral. The brokers, in turn, loan the funds to their customers, typically at higher rates. Although the loans are still technically call loans, that is, one day loans subject to termination by either borrower or lender on one day's notice, as a practical matter such loans are rarely called by the banks. Before the middle 1930's banks typically called loans to adjust reserve positions, and other lenders called loans to obtain cash.

At the present time call loans are more like customer loans but display even less flexibility of nominal rates than customer loan rates. The quoted call loan rate remained at 1.00 per cent from 1937 to 1945. More recently it remained at 3.00 per cent from April, 1954, to June, 1955, during which period there was substantial variation in rates on such other short-term instruments as commercial paper and three-month Treasury bills.

Other consequences of the altered character of the call loan are revealed by the fact that quoted call loan rates have been consistently above commercial paper rates for the entire period since 1936, which is unprecedented in the long recorded history of the two rates. In addition, the rate on call loans to dealers on the collateral of government securities has typically been at least one percentage point below the quoted rate on call loans to brokers on stock exchange collateral. Apparently, the call loan to dealers retains more of the character of the old call loan than does the present call loan to brokers.

BIBLIOGRAPHY

1. Board of Governors, Federal Reserve System, *Federal Reserve Chart Book on Financial and Business Statistics, Historical Supplement.* Washington, D.C.: U.S. Government Printing Office. September, 1958.

2. Board of Governors, Federal Reserve System, *Flow of Funds in the United States, 1939–1953.* Washington, D.C.: U.S. Government Printing Office, 1955.

3. Cagan, Phillip, "The Monetary Dynamics of Hyperinflation," *Studies in the Quantity Theory,* edited by M. Friedman. Chicago: University of Chicago, 1956.

4. Conard, Joseph W., *Introduction to the Theory of Interest.* Berkeley: University of California Press, 1959.

5. Culbertson, J. M., "The Term Structure of Interest Rates," *Quarterly Journal of Economics,* **71** (November, 1957).

6. Durand, David, "A Quarterly Series of Corporate Basic Yields, 1952–1957, and Some Attendant Reservations," *The Journal of Finance,* **13,** 3 (September, 1958).

7. ———, *Basic Yields of Corporate Bonds,* 1900–1942. (National Bureau of Economic Research, Technical Paper No. 3.) New York, 1942.

8. Durand, David, and Willis J. Winn, *Basic Yields of Bonds,* 1926–1947: *Their Measurement and Pattern.* (National Bureau of Economic Research, Technical Paper No. 6.) New York, 1947.

9. *The Economic Almanac.* New York: National Industrial Conference Board.

10. Fisher, Lawrence, "Determinants of the Risk Premiums on Corporate Bonds," *Journal of Political Economy,* **62** (June, 1959).

11. Friedman, Milton, *A Theory of the Consumption Function.* Princeton: Princeton University Press, 1957.

12. Gibson, A. H., *Bank Rate, The Banker's Vade Mecum.* London, 1910.

13. Goldsmith, Raymond, *A Study of Saving in the United States.* Princeton: Princeton University Press, 1955.

14. ———, *Financial Intermediaries in the American Economy Since 1900.* Princeton: Princeton University Press, 1958.

15. Griliches, Zvi, "The Demand for Fertilizer: An Economic Interpretation of a Technical Change." *Journal of Farm Economics,* **40,** 3 (August, 1958).

16. Gurley, John G., *Liquidity and Financial Institutions in the Postwar Economy.* U.S. Congress, Joint Economic Committee. Washington, D.C., 1960.

17. Gurley, John G., and Shaw, Edward S., *Money in a Theory of Finance.* Washington, D.C.: Brookings Institution, 1960.

18. Hawtrey, R. G., *A Century of Bank Rate.* London: Longman, Green and Co., 1938.

19. ———, "Interest and Bank Rate," *The Manchester School,* **10,** 1939.

20. Hickman, W. Braddock, "The Interest Structure and War Financing." (National Bureau of Economic Research.) New York, 1943. (Unpublished.)

21. ———, "The Term Structure of Interest Rates: An Exploratory Analysis." (National Bureau of Economic Research.) New York, 1943. (Unpublished manuscript.)

22. Hicks, J. R., "Mr. Hawtrey on Bank Rate and the Long-Term Rate of Interest," *The Manchester School,* **10,** 1939.

23. ———, *Value and Capital,* 2d ed. London: Clarendon Press, 1946.

24. ———, *The Future of the Rate of Interest.* ("Manchester Statistical Society Papers.") Manchester, England: Norbury Lockwood, 1958, III.

25. Hotelling, Harold, "The Selection of Variates for Use in Prediction, with some Comments on the General Problem of Nuisance Parameters," *Annals of Mathematical Statistics,* **11,** 1940.

26. Jacobs, Donald P., "Sources and Costs of Funds of Large Sales Finance Companies." (National Bureau Conference, *The Problem of Consumer Credit Regulation.*) Washington, D.C.: U.S. Government Printing Office, 1957.

27. Kahn, R. F., "Some Notes on Liquidity Preference," *Manchester School Economic and Social Studies,* **22** (Sept., 1954).

28. Kaldor, Nicholas, "Speculation and Economic Stability," *Review of Economic Studies*, **7** (October, 1939).

29. Kessel, Reuben, "Inflation-Caused Wealth Redistribution: A Test of a Hypothesis," *American Economic Review*, **46** (March, 1956).

30. Keynes, J. M., *A Treatise on Money*. London, 1930. II. Reprinted by Harcourt, Brace & Company.

31. ———, *The General Theory of Employment, Interest, and Money*. New York: Harcourt, Brace & Company, 1936.

32. Kalecki, M., "The Short-Term Rate and the Long-Term Rate." (Oxford Economic Papers, No. 4, 1940; Reprinted in M. Kalecki, *Theory of Economic Dynamics*.) New York, 1954.

33. Koyck, L. M., *Distributed Lags and Investment Analysis*. Amsterdam, 1954.

34. Luckett, D. J., "Professor Lutz and the Structure of Interest Rates," *Quarterly Journal of Economics*, **73** (February, 1959).

35. Lusher, David, "The Structure of Interest Rates and the Keynesian Theory of Interest," *Journal of Political Economy*, **50** (April, 1942).

36. Lutz, Friedrich A., "The Structure of Interest Rates," *Quarterly Journal of Economics*, **60** (1940–1941). Reprinted in American Economic Association, *Readings in the Theory of Income Distribution*, eds., W. Fellner and Bernard Haley. Philadelphia, 1946.

37. Macaulay, Frederick R., *The Movements of Interest Rates, Bond Yields, and Stock Prices in the United States Since 1856*. (National Bureau of Economic Research.) 1938.

38. Myers, Margaret G., *The New York Money Market*, Vol. I of *Origins and Development*. New York: Columbia University Press, 1931.

39. Nerlove, Marc, *Distributed Lags and Demand Analysis for Agricultural and Other Commodities*. (U.S. Department of Agriculture, Agriculture Handbook No. 141.) Washington, D.C., June, 1958.

40. Riefler, Winfield, "Open Market Operations in Long-Term Securities," *Federal Reserve Bulletin*, **44** (November, 1958).

41. Robinson, Joan, "The Rate of Interest," *Econometrica*, **19** (April, 1951), pp. 92–111. Reprinted in Joan Robinson, *The Rate of Interest and Other Essays*. London, 1952.

42. Segall, Joel, "Differences in Price Fluctuations Arising from the Differences in Maturities of Contracts with Uncertain Returns." University of Chicago, June, 1956. (Unpublished doctoral dissertation.)

43. ———, "The Effect of Maturity on Price Fluctuations," *Journal of Business of the University of Chicago,* **29** (July, 1956).

44. Selden, Richard S., "Monetary Velocity in the United States," *Studies in the Quantity Theory,* ed. Milton Friedman. Chicago, 1956.

45. Simon, H. A., "Theories of Decision-Making in Economics and Behavioral Science," *American Economic Review,* **49** (June, 1959).

46. Sprague, Charles E., *Extended Bond Table.* New York: Ronald Press Co., 1909.

47. Telser, L. G., "The Supply of Stocks: Cotton and Wheat." University of Chicago, August, 1956. (Unpublished doctoral dissertation.)

48. ———, "Futures Trading and the Storage of Cotton and Wheat," *Journal of Political Economy,* **66** (June, 1958).

49. U.S. Department of Commerce, *Survey of Current Business.* Washington, D. C.: Government Printing Office, 1954.

50. Wallis, W. Allen, and Harry V. Roberts, *Statistics: A New Approach.* Glencoe: The Free Press, 1956.